Ethnologia Europaea

Journal of European Ethnology

Volume 34:1 2004

MUSEUM TUSCULANUM PRESS ✣ UNIVERSITY OF COPENHAGEN

Copyright © 2004 Ethnologia Europaea, Copenhagen
Printed in Sweden by Grahns Tryckeri AB, Lund 2004
ISBN 87-635-0192-9
ISSN 0425-4597

Editors Peter Niedermüller & Bjarne Stoklund

Editorial assistant Margareta Tellenbach

Editorial Board Albert Baiburin (Russia), Jeremy Boissevain (Netherlands), Wolfgang Brückner (Germany), Reginald Byron (Wales UK), Palle O. Christiansen (Denmark), John W. Cole (USA), Claudio Esteva Fabregat (Spain), Alexander Fenton (Scotland), Jonas Frykman (Sweden), Ueli Gyr (Switzerland), Tamás Hofer (Hungary), Konrad Köstlin (Austria), Orvar Löfgren (Sweden), Ruth-E. Mohrmann (Germany), Peter Niedermüller (Germany), Ján Podolák (Slovakia), Klaus Roth (Germany), Bjarne Rogan (Norway), Thomas Schippers (France), Martine Segalen (France), Zofia Sokolewicz (Poland), Bjarne Stoklund (Denmark).

This journal is published with the support of the Nordic board for periodicals in the humanities and social sciences.

Museum Tusculanum Press
University of Copenhagen
Njalsgade 94
DK-2300 Copenhagen S
www.mtp.dk

Editorial

The current issue of Ethnologia Europaea represents ethnological research in seven different European countries. This issue is not a thematic one but the papers lay emphasis on common political conflicts and social problems in contemporary Europe, like migration, ethnic and national identity, showing the political and social sensibility and responsibility of European Ethnology.

Marianne Pedersen's paper describes how Middle Eastern immigrants living in Denmark themselves relate tradition and cultural practice to notions of identity and belonging. Based on a study among Muslim families in Copenhagen she examines how parents through the performance of different traditions related to three Muslim and Christian calendrical rites negotiate notions of identity and belonging to Danish society. Christiane Hellermann looks at the gendered character of contemporary immigration in Portugal, where she carries out fieldwork on female migrants from Eastern Europe. On the basis of the experiences of "single" immigrant women she explores their daily life situation, paying special attention to the aspects of labour and interpersonal relationships. Katerina Kratzmann analyses different forms of discursive negotiations on cultural belonging and national identity in the contemporary Ukraine and Bukowina. In her paper she describes forms of old and new migration respectively of transnational migration and migration influenced by the idea of "historical home". She argues that installation of national identity through "rethinking history" is a result of conflicts within a society. Luciana Benincasa's study shows how national knowledge and feelings are transmitted in Greek schools. She analyses the rhetoric of speeches given by teachers at school on national days, and shows how images of nation and national character, which metaphors of the nation are produced, reproduced and propagated, how speeches as social texts take part on the symbolic construction of social worlds. Pia Maria Ahlbäck analyses the political role and cultural function of Carl Björkman, leader of the Åland movement for a reunion with Sweden in the context of Finland-Swedish nationalism. In her paper she discusses a number of Swedish past phenomena in Finland in the terms of post-colonialism and tropology. Gábor Barna describes the cultural practice of donating pictures in Romania, in the multiethnic region of the Banat. He argues that donating pictures has particular symbolic meanings of religious, ethnic and cultural nature. In this complex process history and historic experience respectively church and religious identity play a crucial role. Paula Mählck's paper deals with gender roles in the academic world giving a sharp picture about symbolic ways of reproducing gender.

And now allow me some personal words. During the last years it has been my great privilege to edit this journal together with Bjarne Stoklund. But now Bjarne has decided to step aside as editor of this journal; this is the last issue we prepared together. It was not easy to accept his decision – neither for the editorial board nor for me. But we understand his wish to have more time for research and for his family. Since the seventies Bjarne Stoklund is one of the central and leading figures of European Ethnology, not only as editor of this journal, but also as a professor of European Ethnology at the University of Copenhagen. He served as editor of Ethnologia Europaea for almost three decades. He turned this journal into an internationally accepted forum for European Ethnology. He has been an excellent editor with an open mind for new topics and ideas, and at the same time with severe theoretical and methodological criterias. Bjarne Stoklund was a fundamental part of the successful history of Ethnologia Europaea. And personally, I'll very much miss the talks and discussions with him about new issues, papers and plans. We – the editorial board, the readers of the journal in many European and non-European countries, colleagues and friends – say thank you Bjarne for this wonderful job you did during the last decades. And we hope to keep you among the authors of Ethnologia Europaea.

On its meeting in May 2004 in Vienna, the editorial board has elected Orvar Löfgren as the new editor of Ethnologia Europaea. It is my great pleasure to work together with Orvar for the next years. Through his researches Orvar won huge reputation not only in European Ethnology, but also in cultural anthropology; his innovative way of thinking will be an immense advantage for the journal. In this sense, Ethnologia Europaea says thank you to Bjarne Stoklund and is happy to welcome the new editor, Orvar Löfgren.

Peter Niedermüller

ERRATA

By a regrettable mistake the following *acknowledgments* were not brought in **Ethnologia Europaea 33:2**, 'Sleepers, Moles and Martyrs':

Acknowledgments: The following institutions are thanked for their financial support: the Humboldt Stiftung for TransCoop Funds awarded to Fritz Kratochwil and Ned Lebow and used to support the conference on which this volume is based; the Stiftung der Universität Göttingen for its generous support both for the conference and for the printing of this volume. The symposium also took place under the auspices of the Société Internationale d'Ethnologie et de Folklore (SIEF). Numerous individuals assisted in shaping the contours of the meeting, though many were unable to attend, but are to be thanked for their interesting ideas and partial paper drafts: Peter Niedermüller, Andre Gingrich, Gita Dharampal-Frick and Julia Kristeva all assisted in the early stages, and Doris Bachmann-Medick, Dario Biocca, Martin Heisler and Mick Taussig all intended to participate until life's circumstances interfered. Present at the conference but not represented in this volume are Marianne Gullestad (see Gullestad 2003), Thomas Hauschild, Ted Hopf, and Ned Lebow. James Davis, Tatjana Eggeling, Wolfgang Knöbl and Gerhard Lauer as well as John Bendix participated as lively discussants during the meeting. A few of the papers from Reinhausen (Bendix, Marzolph and Noyes) and an additional one included in this volume by Sabina Magliocco were also presented at the panel "Sleepers, Secrets, Sacrifices" at the American Folklore Society Meetings in Rochester, NY, October 2002. All participants at the Reinhausen symposium are thanked for their willingness to engage in the modalities of this venture. Dorothee Hemme assisted in the practical planning phase, and Stephan Gill was our assistant during the actual meeting and also transcribed all the discussions. Karin Ilten helped enormously with the bureaucratic paper work. Jeffrey Beckman was our editorial assistant.

Making Traditions in a New Society

Middle Eastern Immigrants' Celebration of Calendrical Rites and the Negotiation of Belonging to Danish Society[1]

Marianne H. Pedersen

>   Pedersen, Marianne H. 2004: Making Traditions in a New Society. Middle Eastern Immigrants' Celebration of Calendrical Rites and the Negotiation of Belonging to Danish Society. – Ethnologia Europaea 34:1: 5–16.
>
>   In Danish public debates on the integration of immigrants it is often assumed that in order truly to belong to Danish society newcomers need to adopt Danish traditions. This article discusses how Middle Eastern immigrants themselves relate tradition and cultural practice to notions of identity and belonging. Based on a study among Muslim families affiliated with a day-care institution in Copenhagen the article examines how parents through the performance of different traditions related to three Muslim and Christian calendrical rites negotiate notions of identity and belonging to Danish society. Against the background of two cases it is argued that the participation in different calendrical rites in some ways includes immigrants in local society while simultaneously in other ways excluding them. Therefore it is necessary to question the assumption that immigrants' performance of either Arab or Danish traditions constitutes an unequivocal expression of their degree of belonging to different places.
>
>   *Marianne H. Pedersen, Ph.D. fellow, Institute of Anthropology, University of Copenhagen, Frederiksholms Kanal 4, DK-1220 Copenhagen K. E-mail: marianne.pedersen@anthro.ku.dk*

In response to increased immigration to Denmark in recent decades, the notions of "culture" and "tradition" have become salient issues in public debate. The challenges encountered in integrating immigrants in Danish society are often explained by differences in culture, independent of other social or economic factors. In particular, so-called first-generation immigrants are portrayed as burdened by static traditions and old-fashioned cultural practices that impede their adaptability to Danish society. In this way, cultural traditions also become associated with notions of identity and rights of belonging to society. Until immigrants totally transform their cultural practices into more "Danish" practices, in public discourse they continue to belong to their "real home", i.e. their country of origin with whose culture, people, and traditions they are supposedly so deeply familiar. Conversely, if immigrants adopt Danish practices and, for example, start participating in Christmas activities, they are conceived as well integrated (cf. Gullestad 2002:63). In sum, the performance of different traditions and practices in daily life are often used as a scale to evaluate the extent of integration of immigrants.

The purpose of this article is to examine in what ways first-generation immigrant parents themselves may relate tradition and cultural practice to notions of identity and belonging. The article is based on a small study carried out with 10 Middle Eastern Muslim families all affiliated with one day-care institution in Copenhagen[2]. In order to narrow the field of inquiry, the study has focused on the celebration of traditions related to social aspects of the three Muslim and Christian calendrical rites '*Id al-fitr*[3], Christmas and *Fastelavn*[4]. In this article I will use an analysis of how Muslim parents at the day-care institution approach their children's participation in the three rites as a spotlight on how immigrants through the performance of different traditions may establish, negotiate or challenge their families' inclusion in or exclusion from Danish society. Although the data material does not lead to general conclusions, through the presentation of two cases I will argue that, on the one hand, participation in different traditions may include immigrants in local community and create a sense of belonging to the present place of living. On the other hand, the sense of belonging is seemingly limited to present social relations, not extended to the historical community that is otherwise implied in traditions. The data thus question the assumption that immigrants' performance of either Arab or Danish traditions constitutes an unequivocal expression of their degree of belonging to different places.

Understanding Tradition

Unlike the notions of custom or ritual, the concept of tradition implies a sense of historical continuity. Whereas the Latin word *traditio* simply refers to the action of handing over, in modern popular usage tradition refers to both the act of handing down from one generation to another and that which is handed down: information, beliefs, and customs (Otto & Pedersen 2000:1). Hence, when we term something tradition, we lend it authority by underlining its historical significance (Frykman & Löfgren 1996:16). This point seems to explain at least part of the crucial role attributed to tradition in Danish immigration debates. Perhaps more so than most other European countries, Denmark has a long history as a very small and homogeneous society. Even though the meaning of "Danishness" is seldom defined, a strong notion exists of well-founded traditions representing certain Danish values and ways of living that, although modern, have endured in Danish society over centuries. Supposedly, these traditions are now threatened by the foreign and seemingly static or old-fashioned cultural practices celebrated by immigrants who not only prioritise their belonging to other places, but also attempt to reproduce these notions of belonging to their children. This normative perception of immigrant traditions has not really been challenged in Danish academic literature. Instead, studies have mostly treated the interrelation between tradition, place/history and belonging on a very abstract level that seldom explores how traditions are actually carried out in everyday life. In addition, such studies have mainly dealt with questions of tradition in relation to generational conflicts where second-generation immigrants attempt to manoeuvre between the demands of very traditional parents and the demands of Danish society (for example, see Mørck 1998). Consequently, the question remains open as to how first-generation immigrants actually relate to issues of tradition and belonging.

However, as argued by Hobsbawm and Ranger (1983), even though traditions are ascribed historical importance, they are often newly invented in response to changed societal conditions. Whereas Hobsbawm and Ranger discuss this issue in relation to the making of nation-states, it seems evident that also individuals, families and communities continuously re-negotiate and re-invent traditions, thereby ascribing them new meaning and perhaps giving them new forms of practice. Furthermore, in a globalised world where people, goods, and information flow across borders, traditions are increasingly removed from their location in time and space (Hall 2002:9). Several studies have shown how the experience of living in a different society affects migrants' socio-cultural practices and, in particular, their notions of belonging to different places (Pedersen 2003, Salih 2003, Stefansson 2000). Previously taken-for-granted customs and traditions are seen in a new light, and upon return to the former home many find that they have changed their ways of life. In this respect, the negotiation of identification and belonging to different societies often takes place in relation to cultural practices and traditions. On the one hand, families may perform traditions in order to express identification with a specific social and historical background and make statements about membership in a particular community. On the other hand, traditions may also be used to challenge this membership or to establish a sense of belonging to a new place of living (cf. Werbner 1990). Hence, it is perhaps in the context of movement that it is most apparent that traditions are not just passively transmitted from one generation to another. On the contrary, families only carry on or adopt those traditions that appear to be relevant to them – and which they are able to carry on. A case in point is immigrant families' celebration of calendrical rites in public and private spheres of society. Belonging to a minority in a new society not only poses the challenge of finding ways to create and re-create traditions, but it also implies the necessity of deciding how one wishes to relate to the traditions and calendrical rites celebrated by the majority population and thus often encountered in public space. As an example of the celebration of calendrical rites in Danish public space, let us now look at the situation at the day-care institution *Blomsten*[5] in Copenhagen.

Encountering Calendrical Rites in a Danish Day-Care Institution

The Danish day-care institution for 3-6 year old children is one of the places where immigrant families most extensively encounter Danish festival traditions. In addition to their most obvious function – taking care of children – day-cares operate as sites for the making of new Danish citizens by teaching children to function as social individuals, introducing them to a number of Danish customs and traditions, and preparing them for life in school (cf. Handelman 1998:162ff). The day-care *Blomsten* in Copenhagen, which houses approximately 30 children, is an example of one such institution. Activities in the institution are planned according to a yearly cycle that includes the incorporation of new children, learning about autumn, celebrating Christmas, *Fastelavn* and Easter, practising language skills, etc. Being situated in a central part of Copenhagen, the day-care has a large number of children from mainly Arab or Pakistani families. In spring 2003, only one third of the children were from ethnic Danish families.

I visited *Blomsten* regularly during four months in the winter of 2002/2003. The main purpose was to establish contacts with parents from the Middle East, but I also participated in the activities taking place during the preparations for Christmas and *Fastelavn*. Since the majority of children at the day-care are of Muslim background, I was curious to observe the extent to which the Muslim calendrical rite of '*Id al-fitr* would be celebrated at the day-care in December.

However, despite children being absent for the feast and returning with new clothes and sweets to share, the occasion was not marked. In comparison, Christmas traditions made up a large part of the December activities. Children and staff made a Christmas calendar (*julekalender*), on which every day a different child painted a drawing. They also burned a piece of a special candle (*kalenderlys*) every day, and the children spent many hours cutting Christmas ornaments out of paper (thereby also practising their motor function skills). The staff told Christmas stories and they taught the children Christmas songs. The children furthermore listened to Christmas music on CDs and they read books with Christmas tales. One day the children were served rice pudding (*risengrød*) and they later engaged in baking Christmas cookies. The Christmas preparations finally culminated in a Christmas party, where parents were invited to make clay decorations, eat *æbleskiver*[6], and watch the children perform the *Santa Lucia* procession,[7] which the oldest children had practised for a few weeks. Later the children, staff and some parents danced around a Christmas tree placed in the yard while singing Danish Christmas songs. The party ended with the arrival of Santa Claus, who distributed bags of sweets to the children.

It is apparent that the festival activities at the day-care in December symbolically represent "Danish" behaviour, although the children were only taught the practices related to Christmas and not the religious origin of the festival. One effect of the prioritising of Danish and Christian calendrical rites over Muslim rites might be that already at this early stage it is transmitted to the children (and their parents) that you cannot be Muslim and truly Danish at the same time. Upon my query why Muslim calendrical rites were not celebrated, the Danish staff expressed hesitation due to their lack of knowledge of Muslim festivals. They had not been raised with these traditions and hence did not feel that they would be able to hand them over correctly to the children. Moreover, some staff expressed a clear perception that the day-care is located in Denmark and therefore needs to introduce children to the traditions that are celebrated in Danish society. In this way, the choice of practice at the day-care exemplifies the hierarchical relationship between majority and minority traditions in public space.

In the subsequent interviews that I conducted with the mothers of ten Muslim children at the day-care, most parents found it reasonable that the day-care did not in any way celebrate 'Id al-fitr. Being aware of their status as minority, several mothers found that they should teach the children Muslim festival traditions in the home. Along the same lines, all of the interviewed mothers wanted their children to participate in the Danish festival activities at the day-care.[8] Yet to argue that parents completely agreed in their attitudes to Danish or Arab festival traditions would not provide an adequate understanding of the situation. In fact, the mothers attributed different meanings to Danish and Arab traditions, and they gave different importance to the children's participation in the various festival events. In order to provide the reader with an understanding of these variations, I will present the cases of two mothers, Ayse and Samira.[9] The relatively thorough description of the two families' own celebration of Arab/Muslim and Danish/Christian calendrical rites serves to illustrate, firstly, the process of establishing family traditions in a new society, and secondly, how the two mothers interpret the interrelation between notions of tradition, identification, and belonging. By ritualising certain festival traditions, they attempt to locate their children in different "fields of belonging" (Olwig 1999).

Ayse's Story: Establishing Tradition and Identity in a New Society

Ayse is a Palestinian mother of two in her late twenties. She grew up in a Palestinian refugee camp in Lebanon, where she lived with her parents, until in 1994 she came to Denmark through family reunification with her Palestinian husband, Samir. He arrived in Denmark seven years earlier, works in an Arab grocery store and only speaks little Danish. In comparison, Ayse, who has completed high school, has put an effort into learning the Danish language, so that she can soon start training to become a medical secretary. In order for her to follow the relevant courses, both children have been placed at the day-care, until next year the oldest will start in an Arab school. The family does not expect to move back to Lebanon because the couple thinks that as Palestinians the children will have much better opportunities in Denmark.

Ayse is a practising Muslim, and the celebration of Ramadan and 'Id is important to her. During the fast she explains to the children why the parents do not eat, and she slowly includes the oldest by letting him try fasting for a few hours at a time. At the end of the Ramadan she prepares the forthcoming 'Id al-fitr by cleaning the apartment while her husband has the responsibility of smartening up the children by taking them to have a haircut. Whereas her mother used to bake the traditional date cookies herself, Ayse chooses to buy them. Likewise, she does not engage in extensive cooking activities but asks Samir to take the family out to dinner on the first evening. The three-day holiday thus begins with the family staying at home in the morning to speak on the phone with relatives and friends in Denmark and abroad. During the afternoon, they go out to a shopping centre, where the children play and the parents have dinner. On the second and third days, the family has visitors, or they go to visit distant relatives or friends. However, neither Ayse nor her husband has any close relatives in Denmark, and during the first three or four years in Denmark, the occurrence of Muslim festivals therefore made her feel very lonely. Samir frequently works late, so during Ramadan, Ayse had to break the fast by herself several times – an otherwise very social event. During the three days of 'Id, Samir was also at work several times, and Ayse did not know anyone with whom she could celebrate. Since the rest of society did not seem even to be aware of the festival, the event not only made Ayse feel separated from her family, but also reaffirmed her status as part of a minority in Denmark. In order to counter this feeling of exclusion, she called her relatives in Lebanon and also spent one holiday there. However, with time Ayse has gained a few female Arab friends, and last year they together arranged an 'Id party for women and children.

The story illustrates how Ayse and her

husband confront the challenge of ritualising *'Id al-fitr* as a holiday in a country where it is otherwise not celebrated. As argued by Bell, "ritualisation [is] a way of acting that distinguishes itself from other ways of acting in the very way it does what it does; moreover, it makes this distinction for a specific purpose" (Bell 1997:81). In other words, ritualised practices differ from everyday practices in the meaning that is attributed to them in a specific context. Ayse here makes special preparations for the holiday by cleaning the flat and making the children look nice. During the festival, otherwise casual visits to shopping centres gain meaning as recurring holiday events. However, Ayse initially experienced problems because she did not know anyone with whom to celebrate. The fact that her husband works makes the fasting period or the holiday resemble every other day. In this respect, Ayse's case illustrates a general point, namely that the possibility of reproducing traditions to some extent is dependent on the number of relatives living nearby. It is not uncommon that the size of family networks and acquaintances is much smaller in Denmark than in the country of origin, and consequently the social aspect of visiting a large number of relatives and friends is often heavily decreased in Danish society. Among the families with extended relations in Denmark, *'Id* was celebrated in more traditional terms with cooking, visits, and specific family traditions, whereas those families with few or no relatives found it necessary to invent new spheres of celebration. For Ayse, female friends gain importance as fellow Muslims to visit. The lacking presence of relatives, however, does not imply a reduced importance of the family as such. For instance, nearly every interviewed family reported making phone calls or corresponding on the Internet with relatives abroad during the festival. Some travelled to spend their holidays with relatives, whether in other European countries or in the country of origin. However, both travel and communication demand a certain amount of resources that are not available to everyone.

Whereas Ayse attempts to ritualise *'Id*, she does not make any Danish festivals into events that differ from the everyday. Her little knowledge of Danish calendrical rites stems from a Danish language course and the activities at the day-care. Tellingly, it was not the Danish staff, but the other Arab mothers who first introduced her to the rite of *Fastelavn*. She recounts:

"The first time I heard about *Fastelavn* was when Mohammad started at the day-care. The other Arab mothers asked me 'What is Mohammad going to wear?' When I told them that I didn't know *Fastelavn*, they said 'You don't know *Fastelavn*?!' They explained to me that the children have to wear different clothes. So I bought some clothes for Mohammad. When I came to pick him up after my language course, on the day when the children had tilted at the barrel, one of the staff came and told me 'Mohammad was king'. And I didn't know anything at all and she said to me 'Mohammad became the cat-king' (*kattekonge*)[10] and I thought 'Has he misbehaved again?' I only understood a little bit of Danish, but after a while I found out that it was something about beating down the barrel."

The other Arab mothers' surprise about Ayse's lacking knowledge of *Fastelavn* shows the importance attributed by immigrant parents to the children's participation in local traditions. The quote also demonstrates how parents, like their children, are introduced to the practices related to the Danish festivals, but not to their historical origin or religious meaning. Ayse immediately bought an outfit for Mohammed, just as she lets him participate in other events at the day-care. Like many of the other parents, she wants her children to participate in Danish festivals because she does not want to isolate them. However, she does not bring them to any Christmas or *Fastelavn* activities outside of the day-care, and she also does not observe any Christmas traditions at home. In fact, she refuses to buy Christmas artefacts such as chocolate calendars for the children and she also refuses to pretend that Santa Claus exists, although the children had been told so at the day-care. The first year when Mohammad was at the day-care, Christmas and Ramadan overlapped, and therefore she did not want her child to participate in the Christmas party. She recounts the situation:

"The year before last Mohammad didn't go to the Christmas party at the day-care. They invited us, but I didn't want him to celebrate Christmas because it was Ramadan. When I brought him to the day-care the following day, Mette [a staff member] asked me why I didn't bring Mohammad to the party. I told her that Mohammad doesn't understand anything about Christmas or 'Id, and so I want him first to get to know our own festival. Mette asked whether I was afraid that they would affect Mohammad [with Christian beliefs], but it was not like that. I just wanted him first to learn our own traditions."

To Ayse it is important that the children learn to respect Danish traditions, but it is also necessary that they know that these are not their own traditions. In this way, Ayse reproduces an understanding of traditions as a symbol of historical origin and religion. She distinguishes between celebrating traditions in public and private space, because to Ayse, bringing Danish Christmas traditions into the home would imply a choice to celebrate Christian traditions. Like several of the other mothers who have arrived in Denmark within the last decade, Ayse equates being Danish with being Christian and consequently makes a distinction between being Danish and being Muslim. Therefore she also distinguishes between the practices of adults and of children. Whereas children's participation in Danish festival traditions only represents the child's social inclusion in a community, the active participation of adults would imply a religious or cultural *choice* to become Danish. Hence, Ayse's practises both establish a sense of belonging to a Muslim community and challenge the family's inclusion in "Danishness". In comparison, Samira, whose case we shall now examine, is a mother with a different standpoint.

Samira's Story: Inclusion into Local Community

Samira is an Iraqi mother of four in her mid-thirties. She grew up in Baghdad, where she completed a BA in Business. Afterwards she studied abroad for a few years before marrying Mahmoud, a distant cousin who had come to Denmark as a refugee, in 1994. Although Mahmoud also has a bachelor degree, in Copenhagen he carried out construction work, and now he is unemployed due to health problems. Despite having learned Danish and attended different university courses, Samira is also unemployed. She uses her time to run the household and take care of the children, of which one is at an Arab school, one is in day-care, and two twins are nursed at home. Her social network mainly consists of Middle Eastern neighbours, although she occasionally meets with her brother and his family, who live in a Copenhagen suburb. Despite several attempts, she has found it difficult to make friends in Copenhagen, because Danes "are always busy", and other female immigrants often cannot challenge her intellectually.

According to Samira, she finds it very important that her children learn Danish and participate fully in Danish society, including learning about Danish traditions. She is convinced that just as Iraq is her homeland, so Denmark will be the homeland of the children, because this is where they spent their childhood. Therefore Samira lets the children participate in all festival activities at the day-care, just as she brings them to other public events such as visiting Santa Claus in a shopping mall or tilting at the barrel at the *Fastelavn* event arranged by a local toy-store. Unlike Ayse, Samira and Mahmoud also participate in the Christmas and *Fastelavn* parties at the day-care, often videotaping the children's games. At home, the children watch Christmas movies and eat chocolate from Christmas calendars, and Samira makes a "Christmas tree" by putting ornaments on a large green plant.

The children gain their knowledge about Christmas and *Fastelavn* traditions both from the kindergarten and from Samira. As already discussed, the activities at the day-care teach them the practices related to different festival traditions. At home, Samira tells the history of Christmas by explaining to the children about Mary and the birth of Jesus Christ. She finds that celebrating Christmas is not a problem for

Muslims, because Jesus is a prophet in the Islamic faith and the celebration of his birthday is thus one holiday where Muslims and Christians may celebrate together. Regarding *Fastelavn* and Easter, she (like many Danes) does not know the full history or the meaning of the activities. She has mainly gained her knowledge from commercial advertising brochures, local community newspapers, television programs and the Danish language course. However, Samira's story shows how active participation in traditions common to the new place of living may have the effect of creating a sense of belonging to a local community. By ritualising the actions that are part of the *Fastelavn* and Christmas festivals (e.g. making a "Christmas tree"), she gives the festivals new symbolic meaning in the life of the family. They become recurring events that are associated with the particular place of living. Samira does not fully adopt Danish customs since, for example, she does not actually buy a tree, but re-invents one herself. Nevertheless, she prioritises the social aspects of traditions, and although she also thinks that Christmas is a Christian and Danish festival, the crucial point for her is not so much what the various activities mean or signify, but that the children are active participants. Moreover, to Samira, being Muslim is about how you think, believe, and act towards others, independent of whether you adopt other people's traditions. Finally her attitude also seems to be based on her recognition of some Danish practices as being contiguous with her own traditions. Compare her acceptance of Santa Claus with the following narrative of *'Id* traditions in her family:

"When I was a child, in the night before every *'Id* my father came to my brothers and me with toys or chocolate or money. He would put the money in an envelope and write 'this is to you from *Uncle 'Id*'. So my parents told us that the *'Id* comes while we are sleeping and therefore we need to go to bed early on the night before. And [they said] the *'Id* would come from the window. And I remember that every *'Id* I was waiting to see what I got. So now I do this for my children also. I ask them whether there is anything they want or I watch them when they look in the toy magazines so that I know what they want. Then I buy it, and at 4 am I put it under their pillows. Last year my daughter got a Barbie book, and I gave Karim a Ninja. They were very happy, they told everyone about it. [...]"

When Samira lets the children believe in Santa Claus and takes the children to see him in a shopping centre, she simply adapts to a new form of the *'Id* tradition that she herself grew up with. Contrary to Ayse, Samira does not find the belief in Santa Claus strange, because she used to believe in *Uncle 'Id*. When her son Karim once asked her whether there is a difference between Santa Claus and *Uncle 'Id*, she nevertheless replied by saying that *Uncle 'Id* is dressed as an Arab sheikh whereas Santa Claus wears a red outfit and a long white beard. In this way, she manages to use the differences between the two characters to relate her children to different cultural backgrounds.

While Samira wants her children to know Danish traditions, at the same time she is concerned that if she does not teach them her own religion and traditions, a gap will arise between herself and her offspring. Although she does not consider herself or Mahmoud particularly religious, the couple nevertheless try to remember all the important occasions in Islam. They have placed their oldest daughter in an Arab school for a few years in order for her to learn the language, thereby making it easier for her to understand the religion. Mahmoud used to pray at the local mosque, but he has recently started praying at home so that the oldest child may learn the practice of praying. Hence, Samira reproduces her own upbringing in her home. Nevertheless, the celebration of *'Id* differs from what she experienced in her childhood. Samira talks about the last *'Id al-fitr* that the family celebrated in Copenhagen:

"In the morning on *'Id al-fitr*, my husband goes to the mosque. It is a special prayer for *'Id*. It is supposed to be at 7 or 8 am, but here they do it at 9 o'clock, because people should have a chance to come from all over the country. My husband always goes there, and also my brother. Later in the morning we went to *Fisketorvet* [a shopping centre] to see this movie, *The Jungle Book*. My husband took the children while I was shopping. They also went to see *Harry Potter*, they saw two movies. The next day I think we went to McDonalds, I took them to this *Nørrebro Centre* [a different shopping centre]. That's most of what we did."

By re-casting previous traditions into new practice, Samira and Mahmoud attempt to ritualise the 'Id holiday in a new country. It is particularly important that the children experience the occasion as something special and so the couple take them to see children's movies. As also exemplified in the case of Ayse, shopping centres gain meaning as sites where the social aspects of existing 'Id traditions are re-created in a new context. In a cold Danish winter shopping malls offer a place where children can play in controlled surroundings while families dine at affordable prices in the company of other Muslim families.

In contrast to Ayse, Samira does have close relatives in Denmark. However, asked about her social activities during the holidays, she says that she did not meet up with her brother. Since he owns two shops in Copenhagen, he no longer takes time off during the holidays. Instead his wife came by one day to offer presents to Samira's children, but otherwise the family did not share any activities. Samira is embarrassed to admit that her family does not live up to the ideal image of holiday relations. As a substitute for the elaborate visiting rituals between relatives that Samira experienced in her childhood (where elders were visited first), Samira meets and exchanges presents and sweets with neighbours. She is happy that the number of immigrants in Copenhagen has increased, because this makes the holiday more special. She says:

"[…] now it is much better, because there are more immigrants. Before we didn't feel 'Id very much, because we didn't know so many families that we could visit. Now there are more immigrants, so it is much better. You feel the occasion."

In Samira's case, 'Id traditions have changed from relatively structured to more varied events. The focus has moved from extended family relations and elaborate cooking rituals to making activities within the nuclear family and including relatively new social relations in the holiday celebrations. In this way, the performance of rituals away from the original home may not only enforce a sense of longing for or belonging to a previous home, but can also imply the creation of social bonds to the new local community (Werbner 1990:152). Although families continue to maintain relations with their place of origin, with time they establish more valued social relations in the new place of living, and these relations become practised in the domestic and public rituals that families carry out.

Calendrical Rites as Sites for the Negotiation of Identity and Belonging

The construction of belonging is an inherent part of the celebration of calendrical rites, because the performance of festival traditions inevitably evolves around processes of inclusion and exclusion. In the two cases presented, participation emerged as a central means of gaining inclusion. Both women imagine the future of their children in Denmark, and by allowing them to participate in public Christmas and *Fastelavn* activities, the mothers wish to include them in the day-care community. Since the day-care community also represents a Danish community, the two women's efforts to make their children participate may in more general terms be regarded as efforts to make the children feel like and become equal citizens in Danish society. At the same time, the women celebrate Muslim calendrical rites in the home and thus also relate the children to their own cultural background. In this respect the cases show that, whereas practices of tradition may differ and relate to distinct historical trajectories, the idea of tradition itself does not establish or represent notions of difference. On the contrary, Middle Eastern parents seemingly accept the celebration of Danish Christmas traditions at the day-care on the basis of their own experience with Muslim calendrical rites as constructing inclusion and belonging to a society. Furthermore, if we distinguish between the religious and the social communication implied in calendrical rites (cf. Rappaport 1971:66f), we see that in its social meaning and organisation, Christmas is very similar to the rite of '*Id al-fitr*. Christmas and '*Id* celebrations both evolve around the ritualisation of family relations. During '*Id* celebrations in the Middle East, it is common that families gather, special foods are prepared, children are dressed in new clothes, and they receive money or gifts from elders. In Danish Christmas celebrations it is common that families gather in the evening of 24 December to share a special meal, dance around a decorated Christmas tree while singing songs, and exchange gifts. The two subsequent days are often also spent with relatives. Hence, both Christmas and '*Id* celebrations express normative ideas of ideal family relations, and they invoke a moral economy in which expectations, obligations, demands and wishes are negotiated (cf. Löfgren 1993:218). Likewise, in public space, both kinds of calendrical rites are marked by special activities and street decorations as well as by changes in the general atmosphere in society during the preparation and celebration of holidays. In this sense, the encounter with Danish Christmas traditions constitutes a symbolic meeting point where immigrant parents recognise their own socio-cultural values practised in a different context.

Yet, whereas Gerd Baumann argues that in Southall, London, nearly every Hindu and Sikh family celebrate some kind of Christmas at home (1999:129), the case is still different among Muslim immigrants in Copenhagen. As demonstrated in the above cases, parents disagree in terms of the extent to which their children and the family as a whole should participate in Danish festival activities. In comparison to Britain, Danish society has not yet recognised its emerging multi-cultural character, and negotiations over practice may be more strongly pivoted in relation to identity and notions of belonging. In this process, boundaries between private and public spheres of life become blurred. Both cases exemplify that even when celebrations take place in the domestic sphere, a wide range of "others" are implicated as categorical referents (Baumann 1992:102). Practices and traditions are negotiated in relation to family, neighbours, friends, the day-care, relatives abroad, the religious community and Danish society. Ayse's choice not to bring Danish Christmas traditions into the home communicates to an external audience that she remains what she considers a "good Muslim". Conversely, Samira consciously acts to include the family in the social space of those who celebrate Christmas, and it therefore seems that this domestic ritual is partly directed towards "the invisible other" (Baumann 1992: 105) that is made up of "the Danes". However, the two women's practices should not only be seen as a product of their position as minorities in a Danish context. Their own beliefs constitute a strong factor in the choice of practice. Life experience and education may here play a role, but choices also cannot be separated from the two women's different interpretation of Islam and its contents. The content of calendrical rites has a meaning to Ayse that she cannot separate from its form, and thus she only wants to participate in festivals in which the content is meaningful to her. Samira is less concerned with the religious meanings of her actions, and therefore she has more freedom to play with different kinds of calendrical rites in the negotiation of belonging to Danish society.

If we return to the assumptions of Danish integration debates that were outlined in the beginning of this article, the question subsequently emerges: Does Samira's choice of participation in Danish calendrical rites imply that she is now becoming Danish? To answer this question it may be helpful not only to examine the traditions that parents choose to adopt, but also those aspects of tradition that are not adopted. For instance, it is relevant to return to the activities taking place at the day-care. For the parents who choose to let their children engage in the day-care activities, the children function as cultural mediators through whom parents are introduced to a range of Danish traditions and customs. When parents also choose to participate in events such as the Christmas party, the day-care staff includes them in the category considered "active and well-integrated" parents. Yet, when examined more closely, it becomes apparent that their participation may only be partial. Samira, for instance, comes to the Christmas party, but like the other Middle Eastern parents, she does not start making clay decorations. Whereas many Danish parents recognise this practice from their own childhood, it does not mean anything to Samira. Likewise, she joins the dance around the Christmas tree, but she does not know the lyrics of the songs. In this way she is present and included in the day-care community, but she is excluded in the sense that she does not relate emotionally to the traditions that are carried out (cf. Frykman & Löfgren 1996). This exclusion is not necessarily a problem for Samira or any of the other parents. On the contrary, the party may still be enjoyable, and she is happy that the children have fun. The point here is rather that the multi-vocality of calendrical rites allow some participants to fully associate themselves with the historical significance of the tradition, i.e. a sense of inclusion in a specifically Danish community, while at the same time others like Samira can participate without relating to the historical background, but by simply "using" the traditions as a road to inclusion in the present community. The previously presented example of Ayse's introduction to *Fastelavn* practices rather than meaning is another case in point. In other words, through participation Ayse, Samira and the other Middle Eastern parents relate themselves and their children to the local, lived community, but not to the "imagined" Danish community, the historical nation (cf. Anderson 1983). In this sense, they do not necessarily become "Danish".

Concluding Remarks

When analysing calendrical rites as one example of first-generation immigrants' relationship with tradition, it is safe to conclude that traditions do not remain static. On the contrary, the Middle Eastern parents in my study used and re-constructed calendrical rites in many ways. Firstly, celebrations of Muslim calendrical rites inherently change simply due to the shift of context. Secondly, both Arab and Danish calendrical rites are actively used in the negotiation of belonging to Danish society and other fields of belonging. In this process, some traditions are appropriated, re-constructed and given new meaning whereas others are discarded. Two cases have shown how parents may use the ritualisation of traditions to include their children as citizens in Danish society while simultaneously establishing a sense of belonging to their own cultural background. Since the interviewed parents perceived knowledge of traditions as one part of the construction of identification with a society, they let their children take part in Danish festival traditions. However, the extent of the participation varies in relation to factors such as, for example, parents' own experience, ideology, education, and perceptions of religion and "Danishness". Moreover, parents' own possible recognition of Danish traditions as meaningful and equivalent to previously known traditions has an impact on which traditions they hand over to their children. In this sense, new traditions are not invented from scratch; they are based on established social principles and previously known forms of practice.

When emphasising participation in the public celebration of calendrical rites, the parents' attitudes are in line with the official Danish integration discourse that underlines the importance of participation in order for immigrants to gain the right to belong in Denmark. The data thereby point to the necessity to critically question the common approach to cultural integration as a process that has not yet taken place (cf. Preis 1998:12). On the contrary, parents seemingly carry out intensive, but relatively invisible, labour to incorporate their children into Danish society. Yet, the celebration of calendrical rites only makes up one small aspect within a broader field of cultural encounters. Further studies are needed to document the processes of change and continuity taking place in the everyday practices, customs and traditions of first-generation immigrants.

When parents and children participate in Danish festival traditions, they may gain some inclusion into a social community, and they can even construct a sense of belonging to the local place of living. Yet parents adopt practices, but not necessarily meanings. Even though parents have created a well-functioning daily life in Danish society and perhaps imagine their own and/or their children's future in Denmark, they might not relate to the historical sense of "Danishness" that ethnic Danes imply in the practising of traditions. While they may adopt local practices, they do not necessarily feel or become "Danish". Future studies will need to discuss to what extent immigrants relate notions of "Danishness" with the possibility of functioning as capable citizens in Danish society. Moreover, what are the possibilities of making "Danishness" comprise many different kinds of living, and what is the role of public institutions such as the day-care *Blomsten* in this process? The complex interrelation between practices of tradition, notions of identity and negotiations of belonging illustrated here supports the assertion that the social and cultural integration of immigrants does not take place as a linear process of inclusion into Danish society.

Notes

1. The research for this project was funded by The Danish Folklore Archives and carried out within the research programme "Indvandring og kulturmøde". I thank Director Palle O. Christiansen for his kind support and for making the project possible.
2. The analysis is based on fieldwork carried out in the winter and spring of 2002–2003. During this period I conducted 15 interviews with the Middle Eastern mothers (in one case both parents) of ten children in a day-care institution in Copenhagen. The families were all Muslim. Four of the mothers had lived in Denmark during part of their childhood, while the rest had immigrated to Denmark within the last decade. The interviews were (with one exception) carried out in Danish and took place in the family homes or at the day-care. In addition to the interviews, I carried out participant observation at the day-care at *'Id al-fitr*, Christmas, and *Fastelavn* in order to establish, firstly, how traditions related to the calendrical rites were handed over and celebrated at the day-care, and secondly, the extent of the parents' participation in the different rites.
3. *'Id al-fitr*, the Feast of Fast-Breaking, falls at the end of the Ramadan, the fasting month. The festival lasts three days.
4. The approximate English translation of *Fastelavn* is Shrovetide. However, since Shrovetide refers to a medieval festival that is no longer celebrated, I prefer to use the Danish term. To some extent, Fastelavn is comparable to the American Halloween. The feast of *Fastelavn* originated as a heathen festival, but was later combined with the commencement of the 40-day fast before Easter. Today it is a small event which is celebrated in children's institutions and schools, but which is not a holiday. It mainly implies that children dress up as different characters (e.g. clown, princess, Superman, etc.) and gather to tilt at a barrel filled with sweets (*slå katten af tønden*). In combination with the festival, particular kinds of sweets are served and special decorations are made.
5. *Blomsten* is a pseudonym. Likewise, all informants have been anonymised.
6. *Æbleskiver* are small cakes of batter cooked in a special kind of pan.
7. The *Santa Lucia* procession is originally a Swedish tradition, where children/girls dress in white clothes to resemble Saint Lucia, the "Saint of Light". The procession is enacted on 13 December, and children carry forth candles while singing a special song.
8. Only one set of parents at the day-care refused to allow their child to participate in Danish/Christian calendrical rites. Unfortunately, they did not agree to an interview.
9. Since in nine out of ten cases I only interviewed the female parent, I am unfortunately not able to discuss how gender may influence parents' attitudes to the performance of different traditions.
10. *Kattekonge* is the title given to the person who makes the barrel break and the sweets fall out.

References

Anderson, Benedict 1983: *Imagined Communities. Reflections on the origin and spread of Nationalism*. London/New York: Verso.

Baumann, Gerd 1999: *The Multicultural Riddle. Rethinking national, ethnic, and religious identities*. London/New York: Routledge.

Baumann, Gerd 1992: Ritual implicates 'Others': Rereading Durkheim in a plural society. In: D. de Coppet (ed.): *Understanding Rituals*. London/New York: Routledge: 97–116.

Bell, Catherine 1997: *Ritual. Perspectives and dimensions*. New York/Oxford: Oxford University Press.

Frykman, Jonas & Orvar Löfgren 1996: Introduction. The study of Swedish customs and habits. In: J. Frykman & O. Löfgren (eds.): *Force of Habit. Exploring Everyday Culture*. Lund Studies in European Ethnology 1. Lund: Lund University Press: 5–19.

Gullestad, Marianne 2002: *Det norske sett med nye øyne. Kritisk analyse av norskinnvandringsdebat*. Oslo: Universitetsforlaget.

Hall, Katherine 2002: *Lives in Translation. Sikh Youth as British citizens*. Philadelphia: University of Pennsylvania Press.

Handelman, Don 1998: *Models and Mirrors. Towards*

an anthropology of public events. New York/Oxford: Berghahn Books.

Hobsbawm, Eric & Terence Ranger (eds.) 1983: *The Invention of Tradition.* Cambridge: Cambridge University Press.

Löfgren, Orvar 1993: The Great Christmas Quarrel and Other Swedish Traditions. In: D. Miller (ed.): *Unwrapping Christmas.* Oxford: Clarendon Press: 217–234.

Mørck, Yvonne 1998: *Bindestregsdanskere. Fortællinger om køn, generationer og etnicitet.* Copenhagen: Forlaget Sociologi.

Olwig, Karen Fog 1999: Narratives of Belonging: Life Stories in Family Networks of West Indian Background. In: N.N. Sørensen (ed.): *Narrating Mobility, Boundaries and Belonging.* CDR Working Paper. Copenhagen: Centre for Development Research: 27–48.

Otto, Ton & Poul Pedersen 2000: Tradition Between Continuity and Invention: An introduction. In: *FOLK. Journal of the Danish Ethnographic Society* 42:3–18. Special Issue: *Anthropology and the Revival of Tradition: Between Cultural Continuity and Invention.*

Pedersen, Marianne Holm 2003: *Between Homes. Postwar return, emplacement, and the negotiation of belonging in Lebanon.* New Issues in Refugee Research: Working Paper No. 79. Geneva: UNHCR.

Preis, Ann-Belinda Sten 1998: Kan vi leve sammen? Introduktion. In: A-B. S. Preis (ed.): *Kan vi leve sammen? Integration mellem politik og praksis.* København: Munksgaard: 11–35.

Rappaport, Roy A. 1971: Ritual, Sanctity, and Cybernetics. In: *American Anthropologist* 73(1):59–76.

Salih, Ruba 2003: *Gender in Transnationalism. Home, longing and belonging among Moroccan migrant women.* London/New York: Routledge.

Stefansson, Anders 2000: *Strangers at Home: The experience of return to Bosnia-Herzegovina in circumstances of socio-cultural change.* Unpublished paper.

Werbner, Pnina 1990: *The Migration Process. Capital, gifts and offerings among British Pakistanis.* New York/Oxford/Munich: Berg.

Gendered Margins

Immigrant Women in Portugal[1]

Christiane Hellermann

> Hellermann, Christiane 2004: Gendered Margins. Immigrant Women in Portugal.
> – Ethnologia Europaea 34:1: 17–28.
>
> Portugal experienced in the last decade the same shift from emigration to immigration country like the other Mediterranean EU-member states. This article looks at the partly gendered character of immigration in Portugal. Nowadays, many women migrate to Portugal alone, without their children, husbands or other family members; some of these women are the main breadwinners for their families in their home countries. On the basis of the experiences of 'single' immigrant women, I explore their daily life situation, paying special attention to the aspects of work and interpersonal relationships. After some years of immigration, a basic difference can be identified between women, who are main breadwinners, and those without this duty, regarding the evaluation of their migration and further perspectives they see.
>
> *Christiane Hellermann, M.A., Largo Leonor Faria Gomes, nº 11, 2-A, P-2770-108 Paço de Arcos. E-mail: chrhell@yahoo.de*

"Ilegal é simplesmente má, é difícil" (Being illegal is just bad, it's difficult), repeats Tânia. It is a sunny Sunday afternoon in Lisbon, September 2003. We have met after the Roman-Orthodox mass and sit now in a cafeteria in the centre, talking about Tânia's experiences in Portugal:

"Todos que saem da Roménia têm problemas. E aqui, encima mais problemas. É difícil, para todos é difícil, muito difícil" (Everyone who is leaving Romania has problems. And here, even more problems. It's difficult, for everybody it's difficult, very difficult).

Tânia is one of many women who came *alone* to Portugal in the last years. Some of them are the breadwinners for their children and other family members in their home countries; economic factors are the predominant reasons in their decision to migrate. How do these women live in Portugal? What do they work? What is their position within the Portuguese society? What problems do they encounter? How do they feel?

This article draws on my fieldwork on female immigration to Portugal. I am in particular interested in 'autonomous' or 'independent' migration projects. Thus, my research focuses on women who migrate alone, on their own. Those women are not 'following' their husbands or other family members, and their immigration cannot be considered as part of so-called family reunifications (cf. Bedoya 2000, Izquierdo 2000, Morokvasic 1993). In this article, I want to explore some aspects that shape the daily life of immigrants in Portugal, paying special attention to gendered sides within migration processes. My descriptions and analyses are based on the experiences of immigrant women as they are expressed in their narratives, reflected in different social situations and encounters, and completed by my observations and interpretations. In the first part, I give a brief outline of Portugal's recent transformation into receiving society and its current immigration dynamics. By showing different ways how the immigrants enter Portugal, first indications of gendered experiences of migration become visible. In the second part, I examine the position and situation of immigrants within the Portuguese society, and show their predominant marginality due to the connection between their legal status and restricted work possibilities, and visa versa. In the following, I will look closer at two aspects of the daily life experiences of immigrant women –work and interpersonal relationships– and analyse them in their social context. The significance of these aspects for the women themselves will be worked out.

I. Immigration in Portugal

Images of stranded and often dead people from the Maghreb and sub-Saharan Africa at the beaches of Southern Spain and the Canary Islands became well known throughout Europe in the last years. The attention of the media, paid in particular to Spain, helps to alert – and focuses at the same time – the public perception on the so-called 'illegal immigration to Europe', sometimes completed by reportages on victims of human trafficking from Central and Eastern Europe. Portugal plays, within the Mediterranean area, only a minor role in the discourse on immigration to the European Union, largely overlooked similar to Finland in Northern Europe. As a new destination country of immigration, Portugal is not in the focus of public attention and consciousness yet and academic studies are still rare. Nevertheless, the country experienced in the last decade a similar shift from emigration to immigration country like the other Mediterranean EU-member states Spain, Italy and Greece. Some authors call this phenomenon 'new migration' (cf. Anthias & Lazaridis 2000, Castles 1993). While the EU-Mediterranean transformed into a receiving area, only Portugal continued being at the same time sending country (Baganha 1997, Rocha-Trindade & Oliveira 1999). As a consequence, Portugal and Ireland are currently the only EU-member states with relevant numbers of leaving population. However, it is necessary to be aware of Portugal's unique and important role within the European Union: its long Atlantic coastline is the geographic borderland of the EU that serves since centuries until now as port and connection to *ultramar*, overseas, to Africa and the Americas. Additionally, due to its long and diverse colonial history, there are still strong bonds between Portugal and its former colonies in political, economical, and cultural terms.

As a new receiving area, Portugal is characterized by the strong heterogeneity of the immigration flux (Rosa *et al.* 2000): on the one hand, the so-called *traditional immigration* from the former Portuguese colonies in Africa (Angola, Cape Verde Islands, Guiné-Bissau, Mozambique, São Tomé e Principe), often referred to as PALOP, *Países Africanos de Língua Oficial Portuguesa*, African countries with Portuguese as official language[2], and Brazil; on the other hand the so-called *imigração de Leste*, the immigration from the 'East', which began only in the mid-90s but increased fast and con-tinuously. The new immigrants are coming from Central and Eastern Europe (e.g. Poland, Romania), including the countries from the former Soviet Union (esp. from the Ukraine, Russia, Moldova). Also the immigration from Asia (e.g. China, Pakistan, Bangladesh) is considered in Portugal as part of this new 'immigration from the East'.

Portugal has today a total population of almost 10,4 million inhabitants[3]. In the year 2002 lived 413.304 legalized immigrants in Portugal[4], which corresponds to a percentage of 3.99 percent of the entire population. The immigration volume changed significantly in the last decade (cf. Peixoto 2002, Pires 2002): 1991 only 113.978 foreign persons lived in Portugal, at that time 1.6 percent of the total population[5]. In the beginning of the 1990s, more

Russian and Ukrainian magazines, downtown Lisbon.
Photo: Matti Porre.

immigrants came to Portugal due to the increased need for manual labour force (*mão-de-obra*), in particular for construction and lower service work. As a consequence, the immigration rate started to rise until today. If we consider also the undocumented immigrants, which, corresponding to official governmental estimations, might be about 50.000[6], we get a total of about 460.000 immigrants – that means that the number quadrupled within one single decade.

44.4 percent of the immigrant residents in Portugal are women – a fact that is not perceived in the Portuguese society: Immigrant women remain largely invisible in public as well as academic discourses on immigration to Portugal, even if some recent works can be found (e.g. Albuquerque 2000, Catarina/Oso 2000). However, some official statistics on immigration issues, for instance on the *Autorização de Permanência*, tend to be gender-blind (cf. SEF 2001, 2002). Here, a parallel can be drawn to the predominant continuing disregard of women and/or gender aspects in international migration studies, which Nora Räthzel calls "silence" (1992: 29), while Floya Anthias and Gabriella Lazaridis speak of this phenomenon in the Mediterranean context as "invisibility" (2000: 1). A still vivid tendency in spite of the fact that numbers and statistics worldwide illustrate the *feminization of migration* (Geddes 2000, Papastergiadis 2000).

The Entrance to Portugal: Partially Gendered
Most immigrants from the Portuguese African Ex-colonies (PALOP) and Brazil enter the country (at least the first time) with a tourist or study visa, which are *relatively* easy to obtain due to binational agreements. They overstay the visa in the hope of being able to legalize their situation permanently *somehow*, sooner or later. A work visa offers for some immigrants a temporary solution: Barbara for example came from Brazil to Portugal as tourist and arranged a work contract as *empregada doméstica*, domestic worker; after that, she left Portugal for one week to obtain the visa and returned. This practice is common amongst many Brazilian and PALOP nationals. Nevertheless, I indicated already above that thousands of immigrants continue to be undocumented, many of them overstayers, and further regularization possibilities are needed.

The entrance to Portugal is in general more difficult for immigrants from Central and Eastern Europe, Asia and other African, not Portuguese speaking, countries. It is not unusual to pay a couple of hundreds or thousand dollars to 'agents' who arrange a Schengen or tourist visa, or smuggle them into the EU and through various countries to Portugal, in the case of Central and Eastern European migrants. Some of my research participants referred to the risks during their travel: even having valid tourist visa, they might be controlled several times and offered 'protection' – meaning that they are threatened and charged – by different mafia-gangs operating within the EU. The existence and practice of human trafficking became better known in the last years as well as the fact that many women from Central and Eastern European countries become victims of forced prostitution. Consequently, many of the women I met were aware of these risks before their departure, in particular from the countries of the former Soviet Union (Russia, Ukraine, Moldova). To reduce the risk that their passport might be taken away and they might disappear in these 'controls' by mafia-gangs, some accepted rough conditions of transport on their way to Portugal: for instance, one woman spent three days bent in the luggage boot of the bus; another had to cross the river Oder between Poland and Germany without knowing to swim, and experienced then a similar journey to Portugal hidden in a bus.

Sub-Saharan African women arriving by plane face a different problem: they might be sent back if being *suspected t*o plan working as prostitutes in Portugal – even if their papers are in order, even if they have valid visa etc. Officials from the SEF (Serviço de Estrangeiros e Fronteiras, the Portuguese Aliens and Frontiers Service) are controlling at the airports and send 'suspicious' women straight back. There is no information about the criteria for this practiced selection and what is understood as consistent indications or evidence for intended sex work. No numbers or estimations are available how many women are sent back this way[7] but stories of African women being sent back without having left the airport of Lisbon run through the discourses of immigrants in Portugal, repeatedly referred to by my research participants.

Therefore, I argue that the gendered experience of migration starts already at the arrival in Portugal; it continues and shapes the immigrants' daily life as will be shown more detailedly below, based on the concrete experiences of my research participants.

II. At the Margins

Portugal as a new immigration country was – and partly still is – not prepared to receive immigrants. They remain at the margins. Even if the immigration from the Ex-colonies is relatively old, very few policies or programs for social support and integration were introduced. This led to a very visible social and spatial exclusion of the African immigrant population (cf. Malheiros 2000, 2002), including nowadays the 2nd or even 3rd generation: slum-areas and clandestine housings can be found easily in Lisbon and Porto, the main Portuguese towns. And even today, after a decade of increased immigration flows, exists only a small number of services and support programs for immigrants. Predominantly, they are connected to churches (e.g. Roman Catholic, Ukrainian or Roman Orthodox, Muslim) and some NGOs, which, as well as some town administrations, offer also Portuguese language courses – but only few immigrants attend them. The basic problem is that the information on these few existing programs does simply not reach most of the immigrants: a huge lack of communication is noticeable when talking with different immigrant groups. Also relatively complicated, inflexible and partly 'obscure' bureaucratic structures in Portugal make it difficult for newcomers to obtain the information needed, as various immigrants told me (and, by doing so, they confirmed my own impressions and experiences). Besides, many immigrant women tend to keep distance to any kind of institution or networks, as I will explain more detailed below. In the last years more and more NGOs got successfully active in the area of immigrants' rights and protection, despite their mostly very restricted financial possibilities: *SOS Racismo*[8] started for instance in summer 2002 a large media campaign against the widespread exploitation and slave-like working conditions of many immigrants all over Portugal. As a consequence, various cases of mistreatment and abuse were denounced and more people than ever got aware and interested in the daily life of immigrants, including the media. Nevertheless, in his recent report on Portugal from December 2003, Alvaro Gil-Robles, Commissioner for Human Rights of the Council of Europe, refers explicitly to the "exploitation of foreign labour by unscrupulous employers" as a continuing problem within the Portuguese society (Gil-Robles 2003: paragraph 30). And indeed, many immigrants remain unprotected at the margins of the Portuguese society. They are trying to get a work contract not only in order to legalize

Rossio. Photo: Matti Porre.

their life, but also to be able to pay the social contributions (*segurança social*), which gives the right to – at least minimal – security in the case of illness or unemployment. But many immigrants have to continue working without contract, which sets them in a very vulnerable position. Unfortunately, it is in general not unusual in Portugal that employers do not pay salaries throughout months – and the workers are left without any legal possibility to get their money or to sue the employers. At the same time, the work conditions are in many cases (esp. construction work, cleaning service) precarious and immigrant workers completely unprotected: many endanger their health or even risk their life every day.

"Os Imigrantes 'Ilegais'": The 'Illegal' Immigrants
The word 'illegal' is widely used in Portuguese daily talk in relation to immigrants, by immigrants themselves as well as by the Portuguese population. Governmental institutions like ACIME, *Alto Comissariado para a Imigração e as Minorias Étnicas*, the High Commissioner for Immigration and Ethnic Minorities, employ this notion instead of 'undocumented' or alike[9], in the same way the mass media (e.g. Público January 21, 2004). Immigrants are constantly confronted with their 'legal status', not only by the police and other officials but also by the Portuguese population. Here, the use of the word 'illegal' refers not only to the legal status of the immigrants but also to their position in the labour market: the underground economy has a very strong impact in Portugal (cf. Baganha 2000, Sousa Ferreira *et al.* 2000). A significant part of the Portuguese autochthon labour force is working also without contract, not paying taxes or social security. The underground economy is estimated with 20–24 percent of the official GNP.[10] Consequently, the situation of the immigrants is precarious, in particular in their first years in Portugal; for many it is simply impossible to get any 'real', legal job with contract and contribution to social security. Almost all immigrants I met have or had problems with their papers; almost all experience at least temporary 'being illegal'. Papers are an eternal struggle and problem: papers are needed e.g. for staying, for residence, for getting work and a work contract, for the recognition of their education and profession (*equivalência*), for further studies, for holidays at home, for coming back to Portugal afterwards. In the second half of 2003, almost 30.000 undocumented Brazilian nationals living and working in Portugal registered for an extraordinary regularization process due to a new bilateral agreement between Portugal and Brazil[11]. The fact that twice as many undocumented persons as estimated 'appeared', reflects the urgent need for further possibilities of regularization. Being undocumented is a clear transitory situation and is perceived and explained as such by the immigrants. All my research participants are trying to get their papers in order to be able to live a more stable life in Portugal, with at least minimal security. And without the eternal fear of being discovered, denounced, threatened, arrested or expelled.

Work as an Example of Gendered Margins
The labour sectors within the formal and informal labour market accessible to immigrants in Portugal are predominantly gendered: *Men* are working mainly in the construction industry. Strong pull-factors were since the beginning of the 1990s the Expo '98 and the preparations for the Euro 2004 (European Football Championship): in their context various buildings, stadiums, highways etc. were built. Additionally, the highway and railway network is continuously expanded and improved, partly in connection to these special events, partly with the aid of EU structural funds like the European Regional Development Fund, ERDF.

Women work mostly in the service industries: immigrant women clean offices and shopping malls, work in restaurants and hotels (service, kitchen, cleaning), as *empregadas domésticas*, domestic workers, very often as *internas,* live-in maids. In this area work in particular women from Eastern Europe, Brazil and Africa. Many immigrant women also work in the sex industry, sometimes in a situation of forced prostitution, mainly women from Brazil and not Portuguese speaking African countries like Senegal and Chad, or as victims of trafficking from Brazil[12] and Eastern Europe (cf. Neves 2003).

There are some exceptions from the basically

gendered character of the labour market. Immigrant women and men work together in the following three sectors: 1) in the agricultural production, which is mostly to be found in the rural areas of Southern Portugal, Algarve, Alentejo, as well as in the Setubal region in the South of Lisbon; 2) as kitchen workers, immigrants wash the dishes, clean, cut, and cook in restaurants and hotels all over the country; and 3) they work in small (family-) enterprises and shops, which are mostly run by immigrant families from Asia (China, Pakistan, India, Bangladesh), often using extended family networks (Malheiros 1996). These shops can be found in all bigger and smaller towns in Portugal.

In relation to their work, women and men are facing some similar problems: very frequent are an unstable job-situation, which means, as mentioned above, difficulties to get a work contract, problems with the employer, not receiving money, as well as insecure work conditions: no protection, dangerous, unhealthy work, working overtime, not enough free days, no social security etc.

Additionally to these difficulties, women experience regularly sexism and sexual harassment at their work place. Almost all my research participants mentioned sexual harassment; the women, who spoke about that explicitly, work for example as domestic workers, cleaning workers or employees. The material of my fieldwork indicates that sexual harassment is a common and widespread experience by immigrant women at their work place. Sometimes, also physical threatening and violence were told. Similarly common is – also at the work place – the defamation of immigrant women as 'easy to have', as 'open and willing' for sexual intercourse with whom-ever. Some male employers pressured the women to have sex with them and/or told other work colleagues that the woman is a prostitute.

Extremely vulnerable for exploitation, abuse and sexual harassment are women working as domestic workers (cf. Anderson 2000, Lutz 2002): They work alone and have, due to their long working days and weeks, only limited contact with others. This is especially valid for live-in maids.

These problems, repeatedly encountered and narrated by immigrant women, show that the living and working situation for immigrants in Portugal is basically gendered.

In the following part, I will look closer at the daily life situation of immigrant women and their experiences in relation to work and social networks respectively communities.

III. Experiences

Work

Tânia, the woman we heard at the beginning, is 31 years old and divorced. Her 7-year-old son is living with her parents since she left Romania one and a half year ago: she could not earn enough money to pay their living. In Portugal, Tânia works as *empregada doméstica interna*, or simply *interna* (live-in maid), taking care of an 82 years old Portuguese lady. She was employed for cleaning and cooking on the basis of two free days per week but her actual work situation consists of seven labour days, only having the possibility to leave on Sunday morning for attending the mass and meeting some compatriots afterwards – in the afternoon, she has to be back at work. Being a trained physiotherapist with ten years of work experience, Tânia found herself also in the duty of nursing her ailing employer who is neither willing to reward this additional professional service work, nor to give the work contract as promised, which would allow Tânia to regularize her stay in Portugal. Consequently, every time I meet Tânia, *"os problemas como os documentos"* (the problems with the papers), as she calls it, dominate big part of our conversations. Tânia's case is not a rare one; many women migrated alone in the last years to Portugal. Some of them, like Tânia, are the breadwinners for their children and other family members at home and economic factors are the predominant reasons in their decision to migrate.

Many women, who migrate alone, are high qualified professionally: in my research, the women from Eastern Europe in general and many Brazilian and African (not Portuguese speaking countries) women have at least secondary school degrees and professional education with long work experience. The majority of women from Eastern Europe and many Brazilians hold university degrees, up to professorship.

During their migratory trajectory, they suffer in general a significant downward mobility, which has negative effect on their professional identity and self-esteem. Many of them feel that they had to throw away what they 'were' before and feel their skills and qualifications neglected or even wasted. My research participants are for instance lawyers, teachers, and economists. They have high qualifications, a wide knowledge and many skills: today, as immigrants, they work as domestic and cleaning workers – not unusually treated by their employers like "a stupid kid without own will and brain", as Barbara says. She is from Brazil, 48 years old and mother of three children, two of them adults. Before her migration to Portugal, she run her own consulting company, and studied additionally journalism. After the company's bankruptcy she paid her private savings as recompense for lost salaries to her employees; left without money she decided to go to Portugal, hoping that the economic situation there would be better than in Brazil, and also for starting a new life, as she explains me. Barbara works as domestic worker but does not live with the family. She took the job only because the employers were the only one willing to sign a work contract, which she needs to get a labour visa. She experienced her first workdays in this rich Portuguese family as extremely humiliating, and recalls as especially negative various situations when *'a senhora'*, the lady of the house, explained her for instance what a microwave is and how it works, and how to iron. In order to be able to continue, Barbara began telling to herself that she must forget all her past, and should just think 'today' and 'tomorrow', but not 'yesterday' – otherwise she would not be able to stand this work one single day. All my research participants face similar problems with their daily situation of degradation and humiliation. Mostly, they try to ignore and forget about it, their attitude: 'It is better not to think about'. Their self-esteem is suffering.

Most of the women might be considered as so-called 'economic' or labour migrants; money, or, better said: the *possibility* to have work, to earn enough money to support their families, their children, their parents at home, was the main reason to come to Portugal. Being the main breadwinner is a strong responsibility

Post office in the centre of Lisbon, Restauradores. Photo: Matti Porre.

and a burden, which, in moments of doubts concerning their migration, some immigrant women perceive also as a heavy social pressure from home. At the same time, they feel guilty of being abroad, of not being with their children and family. This mixture of feelings leads frequently to a negative assessment of their own migration and its significance for them and their families. One woman from Ukraine, Larissa, sums it up in a very clear way: "I hate Portugal, I don't want to be here. But I need the money to send to my mother, my sister and her kids. And in my country, it is still not going well. I hope I can return soon" (original in English). Saying that, Larissa knows very well how unlikely this will be in the next future.

These women migrate because of the difficult economic situation in their home countries: Migration serves in many cases as a family-strategy. The migrant women have to earn enough money to support the family at home (by sending remittances), additionally to their own living costs in Portugal.

Letters, telephone calls, in urgent situations text messages sent or received with mobile phones, and in some cases e-mails and chats are important media for the maintenance of regular contact with their families and friends in their home countries. Portuguese telephone companies, Internet cafés as well as banks discovered in the last years the immigrants from all over the world as an interesting group of potential clients, and consequently began to direct special advertisements to Brazilian, Asian, African and East European immigrants. In fact, the amount of remittances sent by immigrants is relatively high, more then 333 million € were transferred from Portugal in the year 2001 (this sum excludes international transferences made by EU nationals, cf. D'Almeida 2003:27).

"O meu único objetivo é ganhar dinheiro. Dinheiro para as minhas filhas, para que poderem ir a faculdade, para que terem um futuro. Tudo para elas. Por isto estou cá. Nunca pensei [na emigração], nunca imaginei-a. Mudou toda a minha vida, toda." (My aim is to earn money. Money for my daughters, so that they can go to university and have a future. All is for them. That's why I am here. I never thought [about emigration], I never imagined it. It changed my life completely.)

Irina is from Northern Romania, 44 years old and mother of three daughters. Her husband is ill, and together they decided that Irina should go abroad for some years. In Portugal, she found work as live-in-maid in a family with two children, 14,5 hours per day, six days per week. Irina misses not only her family but also her work as pottery designer – and her creativity: *"A minha profissão era a minha vida"* (My profession was my life). She is crying a lot every time I meet her. Irina never imagined she would have to emigrate one day to assure the future of her children – until the economic pressure in her country got very strong and started to affect her and her family's life in the end of the nineties. Initially, Irina planned to work in Portugal only two years, but already after the first year she knew that she would have to stay at least four years or even longer to earn the money she and her family would need 'to have a future'.

Irina and many other immigrant women try to live in Portugal with the least money as possible, avoiding spending any cent in order to be able to send more money home. The material of my fieldwork indicates clearly how far these women consequently tend to restrict their own needs to an absolute minimum, deny themselves the smallest pleasures like meeting somebody for a coffee (which costs in Portugal 50 cent) and, thus, reduce their social contacts even further (see next section). As a result, many immigrant women feel very alone and useless. Irina's case shows that in particular immigrant women, who have to support their families at home, feel deeply frustrated about their work and life situation. Additionally, most of them understand – respectively admit to themselves – only after some years that their migration tends to be a long-term situation: They need to stay much longer than they thought initially – and for many of them, a return home might become more and more unrealistic and improbable. Therefore, migration and its consequences mean a threat to the personality, the self-esteem and the professional and social identity of many migrant women, in particular when they are the main financial supporters of their families. They have difficulties to find a satisfactory balance between their different roles, duties and own needs. Frustration and resignation are common reactions and problems as they do not see any concrete personal perspective, respectively cannot plan any future, neither in Portugal nor at home.

The situation turns out to be somehow 'easier' for women who are not the main breadwinners for their families at home, as they are not so much *in between* two countries and two lives. Tamara for example decided to give up her secure work place as merchandiser in a big import company and to leave Siberia *"por aventura"*, for adventure, as she explains. She is living since more than three years in Portugal. During the first time, Tamara worked as live-in-maid but left after some weeks due to problems of sexual harassment by her employer; since then, she had different service jobs in restaurants and hotels until she found an administrative position in a Russian magazine in Portugal, which allows her to travel once in a while and get contact with many people all over the country. She is very content about her work and feels challenged. During the lasts years, it was Tamara's advantage, and gave her somehow personal 'freedom', that nobody was depending on her income; therefore, she could leave more easily the work places whenever she encountered problems or which she did not like. Tamara, now 32 years old, is very active and enjoys living in Portugal: she does a lot of sport and attends Portuguese and English language courses, in particular the latter ones for her future, as she says. Since more than one year she has a Portuguese fiancé and they plan to marry soon: his parents are delighted by her. In the next future, she wants to travel with him to Siberia, show him her country and present him to her family. Tamara tells me that she likes changes in life and that she is curious about the future.

Tamara's case is a good example for a personally successful outcome of the migration process and its dynamic. In my encounters with immigrant women I could see a tendency that, after a couple of years of being in Portugal, some women manage to open and develop new perspectives for themselves and their future. Even if most of them have not the possibility to change their job and general life situation at the very moment, they begin to invest in the future and improve their social life significantly: many of these women attend further professional training or start to study (again), learn other languages or open own small businesses. Others begin to teach language courses in NGOs or at universities, work as volunteers in NGOs or religious groups, do sports and join other group activities. All in all, they start to be actively involved and have their 'own' life in Portugal.

To sum it up it can be said that, after some years of immigration (mostly 2–3 years), the difference is striking between women, who have to support their families at home, and those who do not have this duty. The first ones tend to continue like before, feeling frustration and resignation, whereas the latter ones manage to open new possibilities to change their life and future, gaining new perspectives on themselves and the significance of their migration.

Social Networks and Communities…

…as they are experienced by immigrant women, have two sides: they offer support and help in situations of despair and solitude – but they are also a weight, up to a pressuring and controlling instrument. Interestingly, most immigrant women, who migrate alone to Portugal, keep themselves out of communities and more formal or institutionalised networks. In particular single women from the former Soviet Union, from Russia and the Ukraine, are very sceptical about any contact with their compatriots since they encounter an intensive level of control within these communities. The control over women who are alone in Portugal is mostly, but not exclusively, exercised by men, and follows the idea that a woman needs a male protector, as some women pointed out explicitly in our conversations. This idea leads frequently to the emergence of patterns of protectionism respectively paternalism. Most immigrant women alone in Portugal do not identify with these ideas and behavioural structures. Thus, they reject them – and any other control over their lives – actively through keeping distance to these communities of compatriots.

Moreover, these women are quickly seen and labelled as prostitutes. Single women suffer easily from the suspicion, disrespect and even defamation of their male compatriots. The combination of these two tendencies of control and suspicion and a general atmosphere of mistrust leads regularly to protectionism that might be also connected to mafia structures and/or pimping. Therefore, many women from Eastern Europe keep by purpose distance to social communities and networks.

Some immigrant women I met, made also bad experiences with more informal, female networks and 'friendships': also in these contexts, the level of suspicion and mistrust is quite high. Various women from Brazil and Eastern Europe told that other immigrant women, work colleagues etc. with whom they had more personal contact or even friendship, disappointed them because they gossiped about them, telling intimacies or even lies. In some cases started, once again, the defamation that the woman is a prostitute. After that, all my research participants began to keep consequently distance to other immigrant women. One Ukrainian woman sees one of the reasons in the attitude of envy and concurrence between Eastern European immigrants, as their life situation is dominated by humiliation and certain "greed for material things", as she says. She feels alienated from her own compatriots, not understanding *"my own people"*.

Similar experiences of being treated differently and feeling therefore rejected made Astrud from Brazil in her contact with other immigrant women: Being active member in a weekly women's group of a religious community, she has many contacts with other immigrant women from Brazil and Portuguese speaking African countries. As Astrud is the only single woman who is not living with her family, husband and children in Portugal, she experiences certain mistrust and suspicion from the other women of this group. On a more concrete level, Astrud tells that she feels lonely amongst them as her life and problems are quite different from theirs. Unfortunately, the others are not very interested in her problems, she feels rejected – and disrespected. She keeps on participating in this group because of her religious belief, seeing it as a challenge to her own tolerance. Nevertheless, Astrud continues being very lonely and missing somebody to talk to.

Most Ukrainian and Russian Orthodox women, who migrate on their own, do not keep strong contact to the Orthodox churches; they perceive the atmosphere in the communities as relatively closed, relationships seem to be more formal and socially divided. Also in this context many women feel observed suspiciously by some of their compatriots and fellow believers because they are *as women* alone in Portugal. Additionally, some women mentioned again the tendency for being protected respectively controlled. Therefore, Russian and Ukrainian women tend to avoid religious as well as secular communities and networks. At the same time, they also continue missing friends and feeling alone.

Notwithstanding, some immigrant women talk also positively about the contacts that they get through participating in existing social networks and communities. The religious groups offer after all for some women a welcomed possibility for meeting regularly and obtaining help if needed. Especially Romanian women working as domestic workers and live-in maids refer positively to the social bonds around the Romanian-Orthodox church, which is not only a social meeting-point on Sundays but offers also support e.g. in legal questions. Many Moldavian migrants belong also to this community.

In this context it is important to emphasize once more the particular situation of live-in maids as exemplified above in Tânia's case: these women work full day, mostly 6 or even 6,5 days per week, and have only very limited possibilities to meet other people, to get support, to build networks. Due to these circumstances, they are very alone and therefore in an extremely vulnerable position. Since their free day is normally on Sundays, the church becomes a very important social element in their life in Portugal. The mass on Sundays and, especially, the informal meetings afterwards on the street, offer the only regular possibility to see other immigrants and to establish some forms of social relationships. In further research, it will be crucial to question how far migration experiences reinforce religious activities and faith.

However, during my fieldwork I could make an interesting observation in relation to domestic workers, respectively live-in maids, and social networks: the mobile phone, which virtually all immigrants in Portugal possess, turns out to be *the* key-instrument for social contact and support amongst domestic workers. It offers the possibility – or even: freedom – to talk with whom they want, whenever. Without having to use the employer's phone or having to ask for permission. Thus, they can talk without the control of the employer. I argue that the mobile phone becomes for many domestic workers not only an object of great social importance, enabling an at least minimal construction and maintenance of social contacts and friendships, but it is also a special object of privacy and personal freedom. It allows the woman to withdraw herself from her current situation, reinsuring her own identity – which is *not* the one of the uncultured immigrant and often humiliated domestic worker as which most of them feel treated by their employers.

Conclusion

Women, who migrate on their own, experience intensive solitude. It is very difficult for them to get social contact. They are frequently confronted with suspicion – because they are alone – and defamation – often of being prostitutes – by the Portuguese society as well as by their compatriots, by men and women. Most of the immigrant women had very stable and intensive social relationships at home, now they miss close personal contacts and friendships. Many women feel that their social capacity – and, thus, their social identity – is degrading if not totally wasted away. The same happens on the professional level: Immigrant women experience a significant downward-mobility, which, additionally to the harsh life and work conditions, makes it very difficult, to maintain or construct a positive self-esteem and self-identity.

Nevertheless, after some years of migration, some immigrant women – especially if they have not the burden to support their family or children in their home countries – are able to gain new perspectives on their professional and social life. Through getting to know different ways of thinking and living, meeting new persons, they feel challenged in a positive way and begin to experiment. Very often, migration is turning in an enriching experience that develops their personality and identity further. More difficult is the situation for women who are the breadwinners for their families at home: they keep the distance from social communities as well as from the possibilities they might find in the Portuguese society. To some extent they tend to self-restrict their life in Portugal.

My fieldwork shows that many immigrant women are in similar positions with similar problems, but they keep distance to other immigrants – and continue suffering from loneliness. Support would be needed that focus this group of women in order to encourage further mutual help and networking.

Notes

1. This article is based on the paper "Gendered Margins: Survival Strategies of 'Illegal' Migrant Women in Portugal", presented at the 5th European Feminist Research Conference *Gender and Power in the New Europe*, August 20–24, 2003 Lund University, Sweden. I would like to thank the Ethnicity and Social Policy Research Unit (ESPR), and in particular Prof. Charles Husband, University of Bradford, UK, who hosted me as a Marie Curie Fellow November 2003 – April 2004; this paper was revised during my stay at the ESPR.
2. It is important to differentiate PALOP from the diplomatic and political institution CPLP, *Comunidade dos Países de Língua Portugesa*, Community of Portuguese speaking countries, which was founded in 1996 to enhance multilateral cooperation. Members of CPLP are the five PALOP countries, Brazil, Portugal, and, since its independence in 2002, East Timor (for more information, see www.cplp.org).
3. Census 2001: 10.356.117 inhabitants. Source: Instituto Nacional de Estatísticas, INE 2002. Final data.
4. This number includes the foreign residents and the holders of *Autorização de Permanência*, 'permit to stay', which was introduced during 2001 and 2002 and is tied to a work contract. Source of data: Serviço de Estrangeiros e Fronteiras, SEF, Nov. 2002 (last numbers available). Foreign residentes: 238.746 (provisorial data from 2002, processed May 14, 2003). Autorização de Permanência: 126.901 (2001), 47.657 (2002).
5. Data on foreign residents: SEF. Census 1991, INE: total population 9.866.000 inhabitants.
6. Estimation by Nuno Morais Sarmento, Minister for the Presidency. Correio de Manha, January 21, 2004 cf. www.correiomanha.pt/noticia.asp?id=83258&idCanal=9. Also on the official governmental site: www.mp.gov.pt/mp/pt/GabImprensa/NoticiasLusa/20040121_Imigracao.htm.
7. For airports as instrument of immigration control see Miles 1999.
8. www.sosracismo.pt
9. See: www.acime.gov.pt
10. Estimation for the mid 1990s, based on currency demand approach (Frey/Schneider 2000).
11. Cf. www.acime.gov.pt, www.portugal.gov.pt/Portal/PT/Governos/Governos_Constitucionais/GC15Ministerios/PCM/MP/Comunicacao/Notas_de_Imprensa/20030825_MP_Com_ SEAMP_Migrantes_Brasil.htm
12. Portugal is one of the principal gates for the trafficking in women from Brazil and other Southern American countries to Europe, in particular to the UK. Cf. the country reports on Portugal by *The Protection Project*: http://www.protectionproject.org/human_rights/countryreport/portugal.htm, and by the *Netherlands Institute of Human Rights* (SIM): http://sim.law.uu.nl/SIM/CaseLaw/uncom.nsf/0/97f14bbc1f705b1a41256bae004a4de5?OpenDocument

References

Albuquerque, Rosana 2000: Political participation of Luso-African youth in Portugal: some hypothesis for the study of gender. In *Papers* 60: 167–182.

Anderson, Bridget 2000: *Doing the Dirty Work? The Global Politics of Domestic Labour*. London/New York: Zed Books.

Anthias, Floya and Lazaridis, Gabriella (eds.) 2000: *Gender and Migration in Southern Europe. Women on the Move*. Oxford/New York: Berg.

Baganha, Maria Ioannis (ed.) 1997: *Immigration in Southern Europe*. Oeiras: Celta.

Baganha, Maria Ioannis 2000: Labour Market and Immigration: Economic Opportunities for Immigrants in Portugal. In: Russell King, Gabriella Lazaridis and Charalambos Tsardanidis (eds.): *Eldorado or Fortress? Migration in Southern Europe*. London: Palgrave Macmillan: 79-103.

Bedoya, María Helena 2000: Mujer extranjera: una doble exclusión. Influencia de la ley de extranjería sobre las mujeres inmigrantes. In *Papers* 60: 241–256.

Castles, Stephen 1993: Migration and Minorities in Europe. Perspectives for the 1990s: Eleven Hypotheses. In: John Wrench and John Solomos (eds.): *Racism and Migration in Western Europe*, Oxford/Providence: Berg 1993: 17–34.

Catarino, Christine and Oso, Laura 2000: La inmigración feminina en Madrid y Lisboa: hacia una etnización del servicio doméstico y de las emresas de limpieza. In *Papers* 60: 183–207.

D'Almeida, André Corrêa 2003: *Impacto da Imigração em Portugal nas Contas do Estado*. Observatório da Imigração. Porto: Alto Comissariado para a Imigração e Minorias, ACIME.

Frey, Bruno S./Schneider, Friedrich 2000: Informal and Underground Economy. In: Orley Ashenfelter (ed.): *International Encyclopedia of Social and Behavioral Science*, Vol. 12 Economics, Amsterdam: Elsevier Science Publishing Company. www.economics.uni-linz.ac.at/Schneider/informal. PDF

Geddes, Andrew 2000: *Immigration and European integration: towards fortress Europe?* Manchester/New York: Manchester University Press.

Gil-Robles, Alvaro 2003: *Report by Alvaro Gil-Robles, Commissioner for Human Rights, on his visit to Portugal, 27th - 30th May 2003*. Strasbourg: Office of the Commissioner for Human Rights, Council of Europe. http://www.coe.int/T/E/Commissioner_H.R/Communication_Unit/Documents/pdf.CommDH(2003)14_E.pdf.

Instituto Nacional de Estatísticas, INE www.ine.pt

Izquierdo Escribano, Antonio 2000: El proyecto migratorio de los indocumentados según género. In *Papers* 60: 225–240.

Lutz, Helma 2002: At your service madam! The globalization of domestic service. In *feminist review* 70: 89–104.

Malheiros, Jorge Macaísta 1996: *Imigrantes na região de Lisboa: os anos da mudança. Imigração e processo de integração das comunidades de origem indiana*. Lisboa: Edições Colibri.

Malheiros, Jorge Macaísta 2000: Urban Restructuring, Imagination and the Generation of Marginalized Spaces in the Lisbon Region. In: Russel King, Gabriella Lazaridis and Charalambos Tsardanidis (eds.): *Eldorado or Fortress? Migration in Southern Europe*. London: Palgrave Macmillan: 207–232.

Malheiros, Jorge Macaísta 2002: Ethni-cities: Residential Patterns in the Northern European and Mediterranean Metropolises – Implications for Policy Design. In *International Journal of Population Geography* 8: 107–134.

Miles, Robert 1999: Analysing the Political Economy of Migration: the Airport as an 'Effective' Institution of Control. In: Avtar Brah, Mary J. Hickman and Máirtín Mac an Ghaill (eds.): *Global Futures: Migration, Environment and Globalization*. Explorations in Sociology 53, British Sociological Association. London: Macmillan: 161–184.

Morokvasic, Mirjana 1993: 'In and Out' of the Labour Market: Immigrant and Minority Women in Europe. In *New Community* 19: 3: 459–483.

Neves, Ceu 2003: Tráfico humano é um negócio rentável e pouco perigoso. In *Diário de Notícias*, October 15, 2003. http://www.dn.sapo.pt/noticia/noticia.asp?CodNoticia=124781&codEdicao=855&CodAreaNoticia=2

Papastergiadis, Nikos 2000: *The Turbulence of Migration: Globalization, Deterritorialization and Hybridity*. Cambridge: Polity Press.

Peixoto, João 2002: Strong market, weak state: the case of recent foreign immigration in Portugal. In *Journal of Ethnic and Migration Studies*, vol. 28, no. 3: 483–497.

Pires, Rui Pena 2002: Mudanças na imigração: uma análise das estatísticas sobre a população estrangeira em Portugal, 1998-2001. In *Sociologia, Problemas e Prácticas*, nº 39: 151–166.

Público January 21, 2004: *SEF fiscaliza 16 Empresas com Imigrantes Ilegais*. http://jornal.publico.pt/2004/01/21/Sociedade/SO7CX01.html

Räthzel, Nora 1992: Racism in Europe, a case for socialist feminists? In: Anna Ward, Jeanne Gregory and Nira Yuval-Davis (eds.) *Women and Citizenship in Europe. Borders, rights and duties: women's differing identities in a europe of contested boundaries*. Oakhill: Trentham Books Limited: 25–36.

Rocha-Trindade, Maria Beatriz and Oliveira, Manuel Armando 1999: Portugal. In: Steffen Angenendt (ed.) *Asylum and Migration Policies in the European Union*. Reseach Institute of the German Society for Foreign Affairs (DGAP) Berlin, Bonn: Europa Union Verlag: 275–290.

Rosa, M.J. Valente, Marques, M. Margarida, Oliveira, Catarina, Araújo Fernanda, Oliveira, Nuno and Dias, Nuno 2000: *Imigrantes internacionais: dos factos aos conceitos*. Universidade Nova de Lisboa, Faculdade de Ciências Sociais e Humanas, Working Papers 17.

Serviço de Estrangeiros e Fronteiras, SEF, Aliens and Frontiers Service www.sef.pt

Sousa Ferreira, Eduardo de (coord.), Rato, Helena, Geada, Fátima and Rodrigues, Susanne 2000: *Economia e Imigrantes: Contribuição dos Imigrantes para a Economia Portuguesa*. Oeiras: Celta.

From "Rethinking History" to "Rethinking Identity"

Cultural Belonging and Migration in the Ukraine

Katerina Kratzmann

> Kratzmann, Katerina 2004: From "Rethinking History" to "Rethinking Identity". Cultural Belonging and Migration in the Ukraine – Ethnologia Europaea 34:1: 29–42.
>
> In this text, I will describe relevant negotiations on cultural belonging and national membership with the current situation in the Ukraine and Bukowina. Old and new migration movements have a big impact on these negotiations and I therefore selected them as a central theme. I explain how definitions of "the own" and "the other" function as orientations in the transformation of societies, and a national identity is installed through a mechanism of "rethinking history". Migration in the Ukraine goes two ways these days: the so called "transnational" migration on the one hand, and on the other hand, migration that is influenced by the idea of a historical home. To illustrate these two different structures and what consequences they have on the understandings of identity, I concentrate on the discursive assumptions and contrasting natures of the two forms of migration. My thesis is that the analyzed process of "rethinking identity" can not only be found in the Ukraine, but is a new development Europe-wide, which results in conflicts *within* one society, not between them.
>
> *Katerina Kratzmann, M.A., Institute of European Ethnology, University Vienna, Hanuschgasse 3, A-1010 Vienna. E-mail: katerina.kratzmann@univie.ac.at*

In the following text I would like to comment on a process, which today can be observed in a state of contradictory development all over Europe. It is not my aim to deliver a complete history on migration in the Ukraine and Bukowina, nor is it to analyze the process of nation building in detail. My intention is to show the impact of a changing migration on negotiations of cultural belonging. Therefore, discourses and practices of re-nationalization and transnationalization and re-territorialization and de-territorialization are the foundations for the main focus. The Bukowina in the Ukraine was chosen as an example for this text, because the Ukraine is a very young nation. It is at present in the process of forming its national identity, which is something of a contradictory process towards transnational developments. In this situation, ascriptions of "the own" and "the other" are becoming more of a public field that is intensively fought and argued over. The text is written in two contexts: Field observations during a research excursion to the Bukowina that was planned and realized by the Institute of European Ethnology of the University of Vienna in May 2003. Secondly, I base some general interpretations on national identity and self-assessment in the Ukraine on previous notable research that covers nationalism, identity building and cultural renewal in transformation and post-socialistic societies. The Ukraine is part of the Eastern European transformation societies. It is therefore subject to economical and political change, and also drastic cultural and social change. As Christoph von Werth explained, there is a need for an ultimate break with the past in order to bring about political alteration and cultural renewal on all levels. The structural order of things is being changed in favor of reaching a common sense and understanding of the country's future. In this scenario, there are basically three different frameworks for the painting of the future. The first of these is the orientation of the pro-communist era under Austrian influence. The second is the connection to an idealized communistic past with a socialistic system. And the third framework is the alignment with the European West (von Werdt 2000). These three frameworks for transformation are to be found at varying levels of intensity in the different regions of the Ukraine, and can exist side-by-side or stand-alone. Orientation to the pro-communist era and alignment with a European West are found mostly in the Bukowina.

Definitions of "the Own" and "the Other" as Orientations in Transformation Processes

Allow me to illustrate what is described with two examples. In 1992, the Bukowina center at the university in Cernowitz, whose its main purpose is to re-appraise the time under Russian leadership, was founded. For the leader of the Bukowina center, Mr. Pantschuk, the Ukraine is a state that lost its own identity under the rule of different powers. The Ukraine has been an independent nation for only twelve years, and he explains that it is very important for such a young state to define a *new* national identity and national culture. The leading vision for which the country should strive is based on an understanding of who Ukrainians are, how the Ukrainian people should be and which values, ideals and mentalities they adhere to. His narrative of the Bukowanian past is dominated by descriptions of breaks and changes, and he argues that the historical period under Austrian rule can develop into the leading vision for the future society. He sees himself as one of the "original Bukowanians" who were already in the Bukowina when "the Austrians built the first stone houses. And now we have to transport the heritage of a tolerant understanding into the modern state." Through ascriptions of "the own" and "the other," the break with the past mainly focuses on when Bukowina separated itself from the Russian era. In Mr. Pantaschuk's interpretation, the new settlers that came from the East into the country under Russian rule in 1944 appeared to be part of the "russification" per se. These "new Bukowanians" did not know the region while it was under the power of Austrian leadership, so "they also did not know what the Bukowina was and what it meant to live here." They had different concepts of society, other moral values and symbolic rituals for their community – they where "the others". "It was a terrible time," Mr. Pantschuk says, and today it should be the task for every 'original Bukowanian,' as a *real* Bukowanian, to tell the youth about events in history and to create a new framework for a future society under the flag of an Austrian-tolerant influence. The divide into "original Bukowanians" and "new Bukowanians" is very important in his explanations of the country's history. By drawing a line between real and false, he puts "the own" into place and characterizes it. In doing so, historical events legitimize the orientation of the Austria of Franz Joseph, which means it strives to bring the transformation process and current politics in line with democracy. The demand that the "original Bukowanians" want to have "the Bukowina, as it historically always was", illustrates the wish to persuade changing processes in more a liberal direction.

On a different level, the second example describes the orientation of transformation processes in alignment with the European West. I would now like to discuss a daily life conversation I experienced, which is contrary to the narrative of Mr. Pantschuk, who was working, researching and analyzing these matters for almost a lifetime. From it, I found an explanation of how ideas of "the own" and "the other" play a constitutive role in the alignment towards the European West. In Cernowitz, two young female students of international politics tell me in confidence, "The Ukraine is the centre of Europe." This statement is not at all a single phenomenon, but can indeed be found quite often in every day life conversations, because Europe is seen as a geographical region running as far out as the Ural Mountains. But in this argument of the two students, the main interest does not centre on geographical questions, but rather it defines the belonging to Europe (the economically strong and socially safe continent) through territorial and cultural terms. Andreas Kappeler showed very plausibly in his book about national movement in the Ukraine how the perception of what the East is and what the West is changes, and how it also depends on one's point of view. Germany considers itself in the heart of Europe, with its highly symbolic ruins of the former wall between East and West in Berlin. Vienna's self-portrait includes itself as being at the centre of Europe as well, with the "free west" and the EU on the one side, and Turkey, along with a "backward Eastern Europe" on the other. Poland also sees itself on the cutting edge: the catholic Occident contra Russia, orthodoxy and despotism. "But also, a lot of Russians see themselves between East and West: the West, which is the rest of Europe, is shared Christianity and the modern age. The East means Asia, the Steppes, Islam, tartars and the yellow danger which Russia was saving Europe from" (Kappeler 2003: 15). In brief, East and West are all a matter of perspective. In the Ukraine, negotiations about East and West are very diverse, because ideas in Cernowitz are very different to those in Kiev or Odessa. The two young women are appalled when they read the indictment "small Asia" in relation to their own region. This quote does not fit with their understanding of themselves. They exclaim, "The East – that is not us!" I personally am not appalled by their opinion, but I am a little surprised. Being a German woman with my own pictures of "the other," I do think of the Ukraine as being part of "the East." When asked, "And where is the East for you?" their response was, "In Asia or in Turkey. Everybody knows that people are a bit behind times there. The Moslems have more than one wife, and are therefore completely non-European." Pertaining to the definition of Turkey as being "non-European," one can sense the wish to define one's own national identity, which is oriented more towards the European West in order to guide the future developments of the country. One wants to be modern, progressive and forward-looking, or simply – European! And again, historical events legitimize this orientation. Both of the students say, "We fought the Turkish already in 1621 and defended Europe against them. We are historically part of Europe, because we showed solidarity with them." They refer here to an historical event, which took place in the Dnistr region. Guests can still get an impression of the event in a small exhibition within the grounds of the city of Chotyn, which is supposed to be one thousand years old. The exhibition shows, next to a few objects of the rural life in the Ukraine, an impressive painting in which the big battle of Chotyn is represented. Today, myths and legends of the Ukraine as a nation of the Christian West are based around this battle in which the Slavic armed forces fought the Turks in 1621 and stopped them from marching into Europe. The imagination of the Ukrainian people as being savers of a European peace is a clear-cut fencing-off from "the East." In connection with Europe, their imagination reflects the following future aim: to be the outer border of the EU one day and not to be in front of its gates, which is where it stands at the moment.

From the above examples, I can illustrate three things very clearly. Firstly, transformation processes towards political alteration and cultural renewal orient themselves among others through definitions of "the own" and "the other," and in turn influence orders of society. Secondly, breaking with the past and seeking legitimacy of the new social order is established by a "production of cultural heritage". This fact states less about the truth of particular definitions of national identity or the correctness of certain orientations for transformation processes, and more about the fact that definitions of national culture, belonging and leading perspectives for the future in transformation societies function through a symbolic process of "rethinking history" (Jenkins 1995). And thirdly, one could observe that past history, current national culture and intended orientations are felt, articulated and 'defended' as an individual sense of belonging in a personal manner.

Migration History: Systematic Resettlement as a Political Strategy

The migration history of the Ukraine tells a story about a country in movement. Emigration and immigration produced a highly mixed, heterogenic population in which the defining of "the own" and "the other" was not always an easy thing to do.[1] Historically, there were two main reasons for migration in today's Ukraine: the exploration of unknown areas, and political reasons. Around 1900, the first wave of migration caught on in the Ukraine. About 650,000 so-called "fur carriers" left the West (then part of

Austria-Hungary) and headed towards Canada and the USA persuaded by the idea of conquering new regions and finding a better life. In addition, 1.6 million people left Central and East Ukraine (then part of the Russian Empire) and went to the North Caucasus, South Ural and Kazakhstan with the same expectations.[2] In brief, the exploration of unknown areas went hand-in-hand with the prospect of new chances in life and better financial possibilities. Politically motivated migration results in the immigration of "the own," at least in the case of the leading power. The emigration of "the other," or those who became "the other," occurs through re-definition. This import of "the own" and export of "the other" is called "systematic resettlement" and it works as a political strategy to incorporate a territory. Systematic resettlement as a practice of migration is legalized through the argumentation of cultural and ethnic belonging, and therefore has a big impact on the understandings of "the own" and "the other" as nationally defined categories. In the following, I am going to describe this principle of systematic resettlement using the migration history of the Bukowina as an example. It is, however, important to mention that this principle is valid for other regions in the Ukraine as well. For example, fully integrated former Polish people were sent back to their "home county" from the region of Zokal in Galicia. Also, supposed "real" Ukrainians returned to the Ukraine, because their ancestors came from there even though they were already residents in Poland for many generations.

During the First World War, thousands left the Bukowina for official or military duties in foreign positions to fulfil "civil tasks" in the Eastern border territory, and to also presumably get away from the war-zone. When the war was over in 1918, the area of today's Bukowina became Romanian for the next twenty-two years (Hausleitner 2001). This caused an immense drift of refugees in the first few years after 1918. Around 200,000 people travelled towards the West, because they saw their life threatened in the Bukowina. To fill increasing gaps and to rebuild and reform the region culturally, the Romanian government sent Romanian people into the region. Also, to infiltrate their own values and morals, their "own" political, social and cultural ideas, they brought with them their own people. In essence, they practiced systematic resettlement as a political strategy. The first signs of this principle were also in place under the leadership of the Habsburgs, but because of tolerant politics, there was hardly any need for forced migration from the region and one cannot speak of a systematic resettlement in the political sense. Only under the Romanian leadership is the resettlement, or the importation of the culturally "own" and the exportation the culturally "other," becoming a systematic mechanism that is used as a political strategy. This political strategy is based on the assumption that the culturally "own" people, or those who are seen as owners of a national culture with particular values, characteristics, features and loyalties, are transforming the territory. People transform the region into one that is culturally their "own," and therefore *belongs* to "them." The provided congruency from individual, culture and territory is incorporating the region as culturally "theirs," and at the same time, this congruency is reproduced by the process of systematic resettlement, because people are sent to places where, it is said, they always belonged.

The Russian leaders that took over power in 1942 practiced the principle of systematic resettlement and the assumption behind it even further. The population in the Bukowina got separated, remixed, de-territorialized and re-territorialized again. With the invasion of the Wehrmacht in 1936, another big wave of migration followed between 1941 and 1944. Millions of members of the important and influential minority of Jewish people were excluded and threatened so much that they had to flee (Pohl 1997). From 1939 until 1955, many rich farmers, clergyman and intellectuals were resettled in the course of the "sovietization" and through numerous migrations. The composition of the population therefore changed to include more Azerbaijani, Uzbekistani, Turkmenistani, Tajikistani and Armenians. During this time, the "original Bukowanians", whose origins were namely German, Chechen, Ukrainian, Polish and Tartars, immigrated to places all over the world. They were sent back to their "origin", which was not the home with social relationships they once knew, but rather it was an imagined home. If they refused to leave, many were expelled from the country. Through the instrumentalization of cultural belonging, an imagination and interpretation of home was installed that defined an inherited traditional place for everybody in the world – the own nation. It is in the own nation where people have their ethnic roots, their national culture and their cultural belonging. Even if that does not reflect the current social behaviour or sense of belonging, the "nation as home" is politically very useful to justify migration, resettlement and territorial exclusion. "The main task of the migration policy of the USSR was to remix a population with different ethnical groups, to destroy traditional, cultural and personal connections through resettlement and build a new over-national common ground for the 'Soviet people'" (Malinovska 1996: 11). Consequently, the systematic resettlement was indeed not a "bringing back" of people to their origin. It was legalized through the argument of cultural belonging, and was in fact a *political* project with the aim to produce one unified nation. Ihor Czechowskyi describes the effect that the permanent changes of the political, economical and cultural situations of different ruling powers had on the definitions of "the own" and "the other" in the Bukowina: "It is very difficult to transform the loss into a win when the 'not us' from yesterday are becoming the 'us' all of a sudden, and the other way around, such as when leaders are becoming 'enemies' and when a language that was not so long ago official is changing into a target for mockery. For which nation, which language, which beliefs, for whose insignia should you play for?" (Czechowskyi 2002:363). The "nation as home" was constructed by the cultural practice and mechanism of systematic resettlement. Along with it, the idea of the congruency from individual, culture and territory was reproduced over generations.

But, the outcome was far away from one unified, national culture and homogeneous population with similar ideas of "the own" and "the other," because the same method was used by different powers. The political project to homogenize the population and to install *one* unified national culture failed, and whilst the principle of systematic resettlement was a political strategy for varied leaders, a mixed heterogeneous population with varying ideas about belonging and national identity arose. These different imaginations about "the own" and "the other" still co-exist with each other today. The idea of the congruency from individual, culture and territory was pushed through, but with what individual, with which national culture and with what territory should there be a connection? This stays questionable and negotiable even today.

Past Migration Consequences

Previous research covering nationalism, identity building and cultural renewal showed that the production of a national identity and national culture can have different orientations in transformation and post-socialistic societies, but they are basically all working through the representations of cultural heritage as *the* true history (Wanner 1998, Goehrke/Gills 2000, Bahlcke 2002). The orientation of future developments for a national culture, which is based on representations of cultural heritage, is characteristic for these countries. "Rethinking history" is used to establish the nation as a constitutive category in the new society. This means that the country's past is newly interpreted. New meaning is given to historic events, symbolic value is put on dates, memory function is produced through locations as "join de memoires" (Nora 1990), history books are rewritten and new national heroes are invented. The whole process of reinterpreting the country's past is called "rethinking history", and this method has one aim only: to give the impression that there is something like historical *continuity*, and a continuity that can be told in one narrative today. Historical continuity lends legitimacy and reinforces the unified national culture as an "imagined community" (Anderson 1991) that points the way for concepts of belonging and collective experiences within the borders of one nation state. Of course there are, as I illustrated before, different ideas about cultural heritage and which kind of national identity and national culture should be adopted in the Ukraine. The competition between various ideas induces conflicts that are mostly negotiated above the ascribing of "the own" and "the other". As one can read in Catherine Wanner's expositions concerning history and identity in the post-soviet Ukraine, the State is subject to essential challenges. Referring to the Russian part of its population, today's Ukraine is characterized as being the home for the largest Russian Diaspora. These are former Russians who are Ukrainian citizens now. At the same time, almost one third of the population is or sees itself as "russified" or "denationalised". Through these two contradictory factors, ascriptions of "the own" and "the other" are becoming a public field in the current situation. "Many look to the past to understand the present and to shape the future. Ukrainian-speaking Ukrainians tend to see their Russian-speaking Ukrainian brethren as "victims" of oppressive imperial and Soviet cultural politics. 'Russified' Ukrainians, on the other hand, often feel that through intermarriage, mobility, and the media, they freely assimilated to Russian culture" (Wanner 1998: xix). These are only the different interpretations of cultural belonging and definitions of "the other" within the discussions about being Russian. The unity of the nation, especially the culturally imagined nation, is more than ever threatened if one takes religious and national differentiations into account.

In the process of "rethinking history", with the aim to redefine "the own" and "the other" and to put through a unified national culture, the assertion of an historical home is of decisive importance. Discussions about the historical home seem to be distinguishing for the process of nation building in the Ukraine. These discussions support the "discourse of the national", which produces a "symbolical linking between history, past and present politics" (Niedermüller 1997: 247). Historical home means to have cultural "roots", to have traditions and continuity, to have stability of the national culture and to have an identification with it. It means to have security within the interpretive system. The sense of belonging culturally to a "nation as home" comes along with an understanding of "the own" and "the other". These categories have their use in constructing and reproducing one shared idea about national identity, cultural belonging and one national culture out of all the diverse imaginations. And in this scenario, national culture and an understanding of "the own" and "the other" confirm each other and seem to be the unquestionable truth.

I cannot show in this text exactly how the idea of a national culture was modeled in the Ukraine and how it rearranged society. But, it should have appeared obvious that imaginations of "the own" and "the other" are produced through the mechanism of "rethinking history". They reinforce an understanding of cultural belonging that is attached to the "nation as home". In this production of the "nation as home", the history of migration played a very important part. It mixed the ethnical composition of the population and restructured and reorganized ideas of "the own" and "the other", and is therefore subject to the "discourse of the national" itself. Migration movements are becoming a question of national identity and cultural belonging in the redefinition of the national culture, because they both doubt and reproduce understandings of the "historical home".

National identity, as a symbolically produced category, is not only dependent on the production of historical continuity and the unity of the "imagined community", but it also depends on being a meaningful element for the private person. National identity gives the individual a feeling of belonging, an understanding of where his or her historical home is and where his or her "roots" are. It gives an explanation to what is worth fighting for and what one should personally chose as the direction for the future. Through the national identity, the individual is bound to the nation, and negotiations, discussions and representations of national culture are intended to give a template for the sense of belonging. Cultural belonging as an identification with a national identity gives the single person a cultural home, or a place, where he or she belongs. This is to show that the political strategy is no longer to resettle people, but to install a national identity in order to re-territorialize culture. Because the national identity comes along with an emotional feeling of belonging, which in turn fuels migration. Migration does not need to be forced any more, because the political strategy is etched in the person's individual life. There, it emerges as a sense of cultural belonging and personal identification with an "own" culture. It is just as deeply rooted in the character of a person as it is in the territory in which the person lives. Accordingly, a lot of people today relate "the own" to German, Austrian or Russian history, because that is where they see their "cultural roots". Which does not mean that this is where they also see their "cultural home". This is for most people the Ukraine itself. But, to give the "cultural home" some new content, they look back into the past and produce a cultural heritage.

These days, historical migration movements give meaning to the discussions about "the own" and "the other" in two different ways. On the one hand, migration fulfills its task by letting the national "own" become a reality of a national culture, and therefore feeds the "national memory" (Zølner 2000) in exactly the same way that "rethinking history" does. In the interpretation, migration flows seem to re-establish what was naturally given anyway: the feeling of culturally belonging to a territory. On the other hand, migration built a consciousness concerning the fact that there are different competing ideas about ethnic and cultural belongings, for which one can take a position when it comes to the definition of the nation as a cultural heritage. Both the heterogeneity of the population and the idea of a 'historical home' are stored in the "collective memory" (Irwin-Zarecka 1994). This means that migration is part of the "national memory" and of the "collective memory" at the same time. They also have different meanings, which makes it even more confusing in some discussions about cultural belonging. My point here is that the feeling of cultural belonging is not just simply there and is far removed from being natural. Realistically speaking, it is forcefully installed in the society through migration history and the mechanism of a systematic import of "the own" and an export of "the other". Today, this feeling of belonging is saying more about the instrumentalization of cultural differences as a political strategy than about the question of where people belong.

If differentiations of "the own" and "the other" are instrumantalized to a national culture with political relevance, nationalism goes as far as Catherine Wanner describes: "The past takes on a marked salience when meaning, categories, and concepts in the present appear opaque. The past becomes a resource used to forge meaning in the present. [...] I have argued in this book that the unifying phase of nationalism as it is unfolding in post-Soviet Ukraine has hinged on attempts to create a historically based sense of national identity out of the ruins of an internationalist socialist culture" (Wanner 1991:203). The situation is simply not explained with a "rising nationalism", which was always there and was just waiting to rise again from the bottom of a nationalistic mentality. The political instrumentalization of cultural differences signifies a *re*-nationalization, in which the "nation as a home", based on a continuing history and cultural heritage, is used as an argument. Cultural belonging cannot be thought of without the instrumentalization of it, and therefore argumentations about cultural belonging are never just about a feeling. They are about politics and they are about how someone longs to see the *new* Ukrainian society in the future. It is therefore not the only aim in daily life conversations to find out whose vision is the "true" one. It is more likely that the discussions about cultural heritage and the national culture are symbolic. They are a political competition about the power to define the new society, its cultural values, social behavior and moral codes. Conflicts concerning cultural belonging are rarely about the love of the truth of their advocates, but about authority, power and influence.

New Migration Developments: From Historical Home to Transnational Migration

Highly influenced by migration history, there are two contradictory tendencies within new migration movements in the Ukraine today. On the one hand, the discourse of an "historical home" is still very alive, as we see above, and on the other hand, new patterns of transnational migration are coming into place. With the collapse of the USSR in the beginning of the nineties, the Ukraine became an independent state in 1992. The political independency was changing migration flows immediately, and especially emigration conspicuously retrogrades. There are no more enrolments from abroad and the possibility of a democratic process triggers hopes for a better life in the Ukraine. People expect a stabile political situation, a right to a say and an economic upswing, which in turn seeks immigration. Still, each year about 50,000 people left the Ukraine and head towards the West (above all, to Israel, the United States and Germany). But, on the bottom line, immigration was much stronger than emigration in the early 90s. In 1992, the biggest immigrant group, the so-called "repatriates," legitimized their migration and cultural belonging to the Ukraine in an historical home. They argued the same way as governments did, in that differentiations of understanding of "the own" and "the other" are forming a national culture with political relevance. Repatriates, or their ancestors, were originally from the Ukraine and left for a number of reasons to different places and wanted to return to the Ukraine, their origin, when it was politically stabile. This development concerned first of all the Germans and Crimean Tartars, as well as returning workers from Russia. They all referred to their cultural and national affiliation as a base for the current argument and feeling of cultural belonging that justifies the migration. Without a doubt, there were also some who just used the argument of the historical home, while their reasons were more likely to escape hardship and lack of opportunities from whence they came.

The historical migration movements did not only influence the national and collective memory in the country and played a role in debates about the historical home, but they also evolved so that people actually moved away from the Ukraine. Migrants left and settled in other places all around the world.

1994 and 1995 were economically very difficult years, and newfound hopes broke or were questioned. Ideas of a better life in the West were falling on fecund ground. The repatriation was almost finished and the emigration due to economical reasons rose suddenly. At the beginning of the nineties, the migration of the last hundred years evolved into a widespread Diaspora, which provided bridgeheads and networks for newly arriving migrants.

In 1994, this Diaspora accounted for two million people in the USA, one million in Canada, 650,000 members in South America, 4.5 million in the USSR, one million in Kazakhstan and 600,000 people in Moldova. This exceeding potential of networks is dominating the direction of transnational migration today.

These days, more and more people for whatever reason leave their home country, and a new dynamic of de-territorialization arises. Not only in the Ukraine and in Europe, but also all over the world, community networks are constructing "global ethnic spaces" (Appadurai 1998:38) in which traditional ideas of a connection between space and cultural reproduction break open. The congruency of individual, culture and territory falls partly apart, and national identity is newly revised. The decisive factor in these developments is less the fact that "tensions between the global and the local [...] are the prime force of the production of cultural identity today" (Appadurai 1998:36), but that fantasy and "social imaginations" (Appadurai 1996) are becoming a social practice (Appadurai 1998:22). In brief, ideas and imaginations about what's possible for the individual – who to be, where to go and what to reach in life are actually moving people. These "social imaginations" are not just pictures from another world that are far out of reach anyway, but rather they are the "fuel for action". People do think their fantasies will realistically come true, so they are prepared to do things in order to transform the imagination into reality. This process is not naive or unrealistic. Instead, it creates a new social practice. Maybe experiences hold a dissonant reality in relation to the original idea, but never the less the social practice to move that is fueled by "social imaginations" creates a new reality of social life. The individual is guided by different possibilities that tighten the net of opportunities all over the globe. "Social imaginations" can produce a social sphere in which alternative verities about the connection between spaces, cultural reproduction and the individual are conceivable.

With the structural changes of migration, new values arise and cultural belonging is rethought, rediscussed and reconstructed. Therefore, migration movements in the first years of the new republic of the Ukraine, next to the downturn of emigration, are based on new legitimizations. There is no politically forced systematic resettlement anymore, as I showed before, and one new legitimation for migration is brought up in the discussions. Exploratory reasons, which were organized amateurishly and solitarily in the past, have altered into a highly organized migration for *economical* reasons. At the same time, the old legitimating of migration for political reasons, meaning the systematic import of "the own" and export of "the other", is still argued *historically* these days. These two forms of differently legitimized migration work in two different ways. On "one side, the political subject is looking for its own place" and takes care to get there (sometimes provided with help of the nation state). As I tried to illustrate before, historical migration had a big impact on these understandings of the own place as the "nation as home," but now these understandings are no longer politically forced. The individual person *feels* a cultural belonging and therefore does not need to be brought or resettled anywhere. People make sure themselves that they get to the place where they think they belong. On the other side, people are moving in the opposite direction and turn away from their origin towards new localities out of the hope of finding better economical conditions. I don't want to claim that these two forms of legitimation are no longer political. But oppositely, I'd like to allege that legitimizing cultural belonging and the lack of economical assurance can *both* be understood as political decisions.

Now, how are these two different practiced and agued forms of migration connected? The historically argued migration is based on the "discourse of the national" and the economically argued migration is founded on a "discourse of the transnational". I argued that re-nationalization comes along with the production of a historical home. My thesis now states that transnationalization comes along with the interpretations of present migration movements and the deconstruction of the historical home, so that new ideas of belonging and identity evolve. These interpretations of present migration movements and the deconstruction of cultural belongings constitute the "discourse of the transnational". Discourses are not simply the public opinion on some subjects, but orders of knowledge. "Discourses administer and regulate social systems of knowledge and access of knowledge, in which the available forms of expert and daily life knowledge are determined. They reason this system of knowledge with moral and ethical arguments that target a social consensus [...]" (Kaschuba 1999:236). The difference within "the own" country, first of all a cultural or an ethnical difference, is also celebrated in the "discourse of the national" in order to produce homogeneity, a national culture and identity. "Nationalism as a distinctively modern cultural form attempts to create a new kind of spatial and mythopoetic metanarrative, one that simultaneously homogenizes the varying narratives of community while, paradoxically, accentuating their difference" (Gupta 1997:191). The concept of "culture" is qualified to construct collective identities. It designates how multifaceted one country is and which different groups all belong to one national culture. And at the same time, it also defines those groups or individuals who are *not* included in society and the national culture.

The "discourse of the transnational" argues something completely different. In the middle of the seventies, the notion of "transnationality" is at first mentioned in science and is used for economical coherences or technological transfer. To begin with, the notion denominated a sophisticated level of multi-nationality in the course of internationalization (Heise 1987). During the eighties and nineties, the concept occurred increasingly within social and cultural science, where it was used in different coherences. In general, one could destine the least common denominator, or that transnationality designates interaction across national borders. In contrast with the "international", which describes the exchanges and relationships between nation states, transnationality divines phenomenons that are indicated by an actual, a categorical or an imaginary *crossing* of borders (Kälble/ Kirsch/ Schmidt-Gering 2002). Ethnical or cultural differences, as much as the understandings of "the own" and "the other", stem from previous categories, because people with varying senses of belonging share one social space, which they stretch over national borders. The knowledge system of transnationalism does not contain an historical home. Oppositely, "home", as much as "culture," represents a category transformed into something that can exist everywhere (fragmentally produced and overruled) or nowhere (Al-Ali 2002). "Home" has no meaning for the single person, and is therefore not connected to one place, one nation or one "nation as home" to which someone culturally belongs. The "nation as home" is increasingly questioned in the "discourse of the transnational" and other values like mobility, flexibility and networking are becoming more important. "What the nationalists wanted was a 'space' for each 'race,' or a territorializing of each social identity. What they have got instead [...] is a chain of cosmopolitan cities and an increasing proliferation of Diasporas, sub-national and ethnic identities that cannot easily be contained in the nation state system" (Cohen 1996:520). The *one* cultural and national territorial identity in the "discourse of the national" is articulated as many-sided social, cultural and national identifications in the "discourse of the transnational". These identifications are overlapping, co-existing or even contrary to each other.

Let us have a closer look at these developments and how they happen in the Ukraine. In the nineties, one could set the beginning of the development of "global ethnic spaces" in the Ukraine. There was a widespread Diaspora and networks all over the world supported newly arriving migrants. The conceivability of a better life in some other place was coming closer and closer through the media and narratives of relatives and friends, which fueled "social imaginations". It also became obvious that actual and practical crossing of borders rose in the early nineties according to the figures of the ministry of statistics. These figures of migration and crossing of borders increased, because more people applied for "temporary journeys abroad". Whilst in 1987 there were only 85,000 applications, in 1991 there were already 2.5 million (70% of them to Poland). Unfortunately, the statistics stop in 1993, but the border control pictures an increment of border crossings and also confirms the internationalization of border crossers, especially that of refugees (Chabaké 2000). People are coming from Southeast and East Asia, the Caucasus and Near East, from Africa, Maghreb and Lebanon in order to get into Europe above the Ukraine. They choose some human smuggler or are hocked in trafficking activities that bring them from their country to the Ukraine, and then further to the Balkans, to the Czech Republic or Slovakia. From there, they make their way into the western European countries. The border policy of the Ukraine was liberalized since independency, and in the last ten years the collaboration with neighboring nations was solidified. Never the less, a lot of migrants without papers are coming across the border from Russia, Moldova and White Russia into the Ukraine. And the Ukraine is therefore very often the starting point of a long journey into or across Europe.

But the so-called irregular or "illegal" migration is not the only transnational movement into Europe. People are also coming for employment reasons from all over the world. They come as computer experts from India to Germany, as doctors from Russia to Poland and as scientists from South Africa to France. This is, of course, a completely different form of migration, because people have legal papers and no struggle with the border control. They are warmly welcomed in the country to strengthen the "location factor" in international competition, and so that the country can be seen as being tolerant and multicultural. So, it is the socially weak and poor ones who are excluded from the negotiations about who is allowed to get into Europe and those who must stay outside. For the Ukraine, both kinds of migrants are leaving: well-educated ones and socially weak ones, both of whom practice transnational migration. Therefore, the population subsided in the Ukraine from 52 million people in 1993 to 47 million today. A lot of young people are searching their luck abroad and are coming back to leave again, so that the country is loosing its mainspring. It is indeed no wonder that with a general monthly income of 30 Euros, low pensions, dependency on relatives in the countryside and blooming "social imaginations" of a better life in the West that the young are leaving the Ukraine. These developments show that people are still making their way to Diaspora members or relatives abroad to stay there and build up a new life. But more and more people are not actually emigrating, but moving back and forth. They move to a foreign country for some time, come back to the Ukraine and move somewhere else again. These migration movements are creating so called "transnational social spaces" (Pries 1998). Stephen Castles and Mark Miller showed how migration rose since the eighties (Castles/Miller 1993: 4), and in the year 1992, the International Migration Organization accounted for one hundred million people living outside their native country. The directions of international migration changed quite a bit since the sixties, from the traditional movements from the North to the South, towards movements from Africa, Asia, South America and Russia to the industrialized regions. After the cold war the feared stream from the East did not arrive in Europe, but a multi-layered system of commuter traffic is slowly coming into being. An expanding international labor market for highly qualified workers functions as a multiplication factor for transnational migration movements, and leaves some countries with a brain drain. Global cities as centers of production, capital investment and "places of hybridism" (Sassen 2001) are magnets for working forces, no matter if they're highly qualified or not. And some authors like Ludger Pries and others think it is justifiable to speak about a new era of migration (Pries 1998; Castles/Miller 1993). Next to changes regarding quantity and quality, as much as destination routes and reasons of migration, another attending phenomenon of the new transnational migration is recognized. This is the accruement of "transnational social spaces". These are characterized by transnationality in a twin sense. On the one hand, spaces as ways, rivers or passages develop between the places of migration, and can be used by all sorts of people. On the other hand, spaces are locations, places or niches, which are minted by the attendance of several nationalities. This means that common explanation patterns are no longer sufficient enough. There is no longer "a procedure of sallying, arriving and (at least in the second generation) integrating in the host country [...]. The phenomenon is also not properly explained as a process of building a new ethnic minority or Diaspora [...]. In point of fact, new social realities (norms for actions, cultural environment, local economic settings, social networks, etc.) are built, which transform the former social context of the state of origin and the state of arrival qualitatively. They also stretch themselves as new social spaces in between and above these two contexts" (Pries 1998: 63). In brief, the individual can have social relations with several localities. People commute over national borders and therefore create connections between the visited places. They are neither tourists, who leave after some time and return to their home country, nor are they migrants who integrate more or less in the new society in order to stay steadily. With their presence in two or more social contexts, they are "transmigrants".

All together, the Ukraine is still partially incomplete in its migration control through legislative and administrative structures. Laws and rules concerning the migration were carried out slowly in the last ten years and came along with the endeavor to install structured deportation machinery. With the continuing process of Europeanization and the Ukraine standing on Europe's doorstep, migration and its control are becoming more and more important. Currently, it can take up to six months to get a Ukrainian passport in order to stop people from leaving and there are serious concerns about the future developments. International organizations are working on an "institution-building" with the government and questions about migration and refugees are cogitated (Forschungsgesellschaft Flucht und Migration 1997). Not to mention the difficulties of a nation that is still in the building-up process, and therefore can hardly cope with questioning nation state principles. National and cultural identifications break open in favor of alternative ideas that develop in the "transnational social spaces". What happens to the understanding of identity and identifications in this contradictory expansion of social, cultural, political and economical life?

New Migration Consequences

If one understands the discourses about nation, culture and belonging as organizations of space that produce ways and localities as "transnational social spaces," then transnationalism appears to be the countermovement to the conventional national organizations of space. Space is getting restructured in an alternative way and this restructuring retroacts the understandings of cultural belonging and identity. New identifications, or at least the possibility to differ from one national identity and the reproduction of "the own" as culturally belonging to a national culture, are given (Gupta/Ferguson 1997). As a characterization of the new spaces, which are currently arising all over Europe and not just in the Ukraine (meaning *across* the Ukraine and neighboring states), one can stress two points. A high level of specifying networks and transnationalism, in the twin sense as I explained before, both open up ideas and ascriptions of "the own" and "the other." The attempt to produce one emotionally bound nation as a collective experience through representations of a cultural heritage and the process of "rethinking history" is in discord with the development of "transnational social spaces". Therefore, different understandings of identity, belonging and nation exist in one country. And these are not just differences about which nation someone feels for or belongs to, but about the whole *concept* of belonging. Obviously, by courtesy of people from various national countries using ways and localities mutually, a new dynamic takes place in the "transnational social spaces." This dynamic has the potential to rethink cultural, social, political and economical belongings and negotiations, and to reinterpret them in new ways. In these new spaces, belongings are still often articulated as a national matter, but through a common social practice, alternate thinking models and templates for solidarity, values and ethic patterns grow. Traditional understandings of a "nation as home" and former definitions of "the own" and "the other" are convulsed, which accrues an essential contradiction. On the one side, it is a matter of fact that "the imagination of community and society [...] functions through codes of inclusion and exclusion" (Imhof 2002). And on the other side, these codes are questioned and threatened by transnational migration and the new developments of "transnational social spaces."

The new forms of migration are bringing about a dialectic field between the "discourse of the national" and the "discourse of the transnational", and this is what makes the determination of one unified national culture very difficult. Insecurities about the value and use of cultural belonging in the old sense and about where to go, what to do and who to be are taking over. New identities arise and "such identities escape from either-or classification and become defined more by a logic of "both-and-and," in which the subject shares partial overlapping identities with other similarly constituted decentered subjects that inhabit reticular social forms" (Kearny 1995:558). Hybrid, multiple or multilocal identities bulge out, and those identification concepts which are based on the congruency of individual, culture and territory, don't seem to meet reality anymore. The success story of the nation state as the founder of identity suffers through the new "transnational social spaces" of the transnational migration. New social practices and alternative models of identification irritate national understandings of belonging, and therefore new ideas about belonging are developing in the process of "rethinking identity". These new ideas still see people as citizens of nation states and don't deny their national membership, but they also see people as members in other small or big units of belonging. There is not only one national culture and one national identity, but also rather a concept of belonging as a multiple subject who is a member of diverse collectives. If transnational migration processes irritate the collective founding identities of a nation, then new answers need to be found to the question of how to deal with the fact of not having an unequivocal national belonging as a cultural identity. Let's not forget that new identifications can be experienced differently. The cultural and social attendance in two or more places and contexts mean different things for different people. For some, it might be enrichment and for others it is a trigger of insecurity and fear. There are no rules, and the perception of the situation is as multiple as the people are: they can stick with the "discourse of the national" or be against it, and they can have resistance against the "discourse of the transnational" or be in line with it. Or, they can make up their own mixture of different arguments of both the discourses.

In this specific situation, one can comprehend developments all over Europe, which are of importance for all nation states. On the one hand, there are transnational movements in migration, economy, institutions, finances, plus social and business networks. On the other hand, there are efforts to refasten the nation state, and to secure its authority, sovereignty and power. The strengthening principles of the nation state contradict the dissolving ones. The widespread picture in Europe from a people as one "Volkskörper", the leviathan as one unified nation, and a single body with a special character and mentality, is questionable. And as we could see from the example of the Ukraine, contradictory forces are tugging on some states. In the Ukraine the attempt to import "the own" and export "the other" (based on a national culture and identity) failed and switched completely, because it was practiced by different political powers. Not one unified nation comes out of this history, but a country with a heterogenic population that has varying and sometimes competing ideas about cultural belonging and who "the other" is. This heterogenic population is confronted with the phenomenon of transnational movements, which mixes the understanding and negotiations of cultural belonging up even more. "The own" in cultural terms or as a national culture is not existent in the "discourse of the transnational", and therefore a national identity needs to be reproduced in the "discourse of the national" to delimitate the putative "other". This might explain targets of nationalistic oriented groups today to some extent, but the fundamental problem cannot be solved. In a nation state with varying imaginations of social, cultural and economic belongings, everybody fights against *another* "the other". And dissociations, as well as processes of exclusion, are not only taking place at the national borders, but *amidst* society.

The two described discourses of the national and transnational both produce a discursive space that is colliding in the different ways of behavior and thinking. Both discourses are trying to put their truths through to a social reality in order to gain as much control and power in society as they can. Like we saw at the beginning of the text, the goal of some Bukowanians is to define a cultural belonging to Europe above the territorial and historical connection. And this is only one way amongst a few that could be used to guide future orientations. But, in all European states we can find the tendency that the linkage between the individual, cultural and territorial belonging breaks open in the process of de-territorializiation. Contemporaneously, this linkage gets reproduced in negotiations about "the own" and "the other" in the process of re-territorialization. The process of "rethinking history" is not to be found in all states. Most of the European states already enact a long tradition of their national references. But, I would like to add that in almost all states one can observe transnational migration and other transnational movements that have consequences on the understanding of cultural belonging and affiliation. "Rethinking identity" is a European-wide process that takes part in the dialectic field of renationalization and transnationalization, in between the "discourse of the national" and the "discourse of the transnational."

Notes

1. Further information about migration in the Ukraine of single ethnic groups or specific themes can be found in the three institutions for research about migration in Kiev: *National Institute for strategic research of the Ukraine, Centre for population studies at the national University in Kiev* (www.univ.kiev.ua), *Section for working migration and socio-economic prediction of working forces at the research centre for employment and labour market problems.*
2. The following statistics are from the study by Olena Malinovska: *Migration und Migrationspolitik in der Ukraine nach 1991. Berichte des Bundesinstituts für ostwissenschaftliche und internationale Studien.* Köln 1996. The numbers and statistics in this source are taken from the main source of the ministry for statistics in the Ukraine. They are to be taken with circumspection, because some of them rely on documents and not on real entry in or exit out of the country and are therefore unreliable.

References

Anderson, Benedict 1991: *Imagined Communities: reflections on the origin and spread of nationalism*. London: Verso.

Al-Ali, Nadje Sadig (ed.) 2002: *New approaches to migration? Transnational communities and the transformation of home*. London: Routledge.

Appadurai, Arjun 1996: *Modernity at Large*. Minneapolis: Univ. of Minnesota Press.

Appadurai, Arjun 1998: Globale ethnische Räume. Bemerkungen und Fragen zur Entwicklung einer transnationalen Anthropologie. In: Ulrich Beck (ed.): *Perspektiven der Weltgesellschaft*. Frankfurt am Main: Suhrkamp. 11–40.

Bahlcke, Joachim (ed.) 2002: *Die Konstruktion der Vergangenheit: Geschichtsdenken, Traditionsbildung und Selbstdarstellung im frühneuzeitlichen Ostmitteleuropas*. Berlin: Duncker & Humblot.

Besters-Dilger, Juliane (ed.) 2003: *Die Ukraine in Europa. Aktuelle Lage, Hintergründe und Perspektiven*. Wien, Köln, Weimar: Böhlau.

Castles, Stephen/ Miller, Mark J. 1993: *The age of migration: International population movements in the modern world*. New York: Guilford Press.

Chabaké, Tarek Armando Abou 2000: Irreguläre Migration und Schleusertum: Im Wechselspiel von Legalität und Illegalität. In: *Historische Sozialkunde*, Bd. 17: Internationale Entwicklung. Frankfurt am Main: Brandes & Apsel. 123–144.

Cohen, Robin 1996: Diasporas and the nation-state: from victims to challengers. In: *International Affairs* 72, 3. Moskau. 507–520.

Czechowskyi, Ihor 2002: Das "Chernowitzer Schiff": Unter dem Segel der Toleranz in ein vereintes Europa. In: Cordon, Cécile / Kusdat, Helmut: *An der Zeiten Ränder. Czernowitz und die Bukowina. Geschichte, Literatur, Verfolgung, Exil*. Wien: Theodor-Kramer-Ges. 361–380.

Forschungsgesellschaft Flucht und Migration 1997: *Ukraine: Vor den Toren Europas – Die Vorverlagerung der Abschottungspolitik*. Heft 5 der FFM-Reihe. Berlin: Schwarze Risse.

Goehrke, Carsten/ Gills, Seraina 2000: *Transformation und historisches Erbe in den Staaten des europäischen Ostens*. Wien, Bern: Lang.

Gupta, Akhil 1997: The Song of the Nonaligned World: Transnational Identities and the Reinscription od Space in Late Capitalism. In: Gupta, Akhil/ Ferguson, James: *Culture, Power, Place. Explorations in critical anthropology*. Durham, NC: Duke Univ. Press. 179–199.

Gupta, Akhil/ Ferguson, James 1997: *Culture, Power, Place. Explorations in critical anthropology*. Durham, NC: Duke Univ. Press.

Hausleitner, Mariana 2001: *Die Rumänisierung der Bukowina. Die Durchsetzung des nationalstaatlichen Anspruchs Großrumäniens 1918–1944*. München: Oldenbourg.

Heise, Heinz-Joachim 1987: *Probleme der Transnationalisierung japanischer Unternehmen*. Berlin.

Imhof, Kurt 2002: Öffentlichkeit und Identität. In: Kälble, Hartmut / Kirsch, Martin / Schmidt-Gernig, Alexander (eds.): *Transnationale Öffentlichkeiten und Identitäten im 20. Jahrhundert*. Frankfurt am Main: Campus. 37–56.

Irwin-Zarecka, Iwona 1994: *Frames of remembrance: the dynamics of collective memory*. New Brunswick, NJ [u.a.]: Transaction Publication.

Jenkins, Keith 1995: *Re-thinking History*. London: Routledge.

Kälble, Hartmut/ Kirsch, Martin/ Schmidt-Gernig, Alexander (eds.) 2002: *Zur Entwicklung transnationaler Öffentlichkeiten und Identitäten im 20. Jahrhundert*. Frankfurt am Main: Campus.

Kappeler, Andreas 2003: *Der schwierige Weg zur Nation. Beiträge zur neueren Geschichte der Ukraine*. Wien, Köln, Weimar: Böhlau.

Kaschuba, Wolfgang 1999: *Einführung in die Europäische Ethnologie*. München: C.H.Beck.

Kearney, Michael 1995: The Local and the Global: The Anthropology of Globalisation and Transnationalism. In: *Annual Review of Anthropology*, 24. Palo Alto: Annual Review Inc. 547–566.

Malinovska, Olena 1996: *Migration und Migrationspolitik in der Ukraine nach 1991*. Berichte des Bundesinstituts für ostwissenschaftliche und internationale Studien. Köln.

Müller-Funk, Wolfgang/ Plener, Peter/ Ruthner, Clemens (eds.) 2002: *Kakanien revisited. das Eigene und das Fremde in der österreichisch-ungarischen Monarchie*. Tübingen: Francke.

Niedermüller, Peter 1997: Zeit, Geschichte, Vergangenheit. Zur kulturellen Logik des Nationalismus im Postsozialismus. In: *Historische Anthropologie. Kultur, Gesellschaft, Alltag*. Köln, Weimar, Wien: Böhlau. 5.Jahrgang, Heft 1, 245–267.

Nora, Pierre 1990: '*Zwischen Geschichte und Gedächtnis*. Berlin: Wagenbach.

Pohl, Dieter 1996: *Nationalsozialistische Judenverfolgung in Ostgalizien 1941–44: Organisation und Durchführung eines staatlichen Massenverbrechens*. München: Oldenbourg. (Studien zur Zeitgeschichte).

Pries, Ludger 1998: Transnationale soziale Räume. In: Beck, Ulrich (ed.): *Perspektiven der Weltgesellschaft*. Frankfurt am Main: Suhrkamp. 55–86.

Sassen, Saskia 2001: *Global Cities*. 2.ed. New York, London, Tokyo: Princeton Univ. Press.

von Werdt, Christoph 2000: Transformation und nationale Identität in der Ukraine und in Belarus. Ein historischer Vergleich. In: Goehrke, Carsten/ Gills, Seraina: *Transformation und historisches Erbe in den Staaten des europäischen Ostens*. Wien, Bern: Lang. 331–364.

Wanner, Catherine 1998: *Burden of Dreams: History and Identity in Post-Soviet Ukraine*. Pennsylvania State University.

Zølner, Mette 2000: *Re-imagining the nation : debates on immigrants, identities and memories*. Brüssel, Wien: PIE Lang.

"History is the Mirror of Our Character"
National Character in Greek Teachers' Speeches on National Day Commemorations

Luciana Benincasa

> Benincasa, Luciana 2004: "History is the Mirror of Our Character": National Character in Greek Teachers' Speeches on National Day Commemorations. – Ethnologia Europaea 34:1: 43–60.
>
> The paper analyses some aspects of the speeches that Greek teachers give at school on national days. A view of the nation as a "natural unit" becomes the basis for the alleged "national character." The nation's past struggles are presented as the natural consequence of national character. In this way national character becomes destiny. At the same time, though, heroic behaviour may influence fate and succeed in altering that destiny, when it is felt as unjust. Speeches given on national day commemorations (a) confirm and consecrate a model of the world as consisting of discrete nations, each with a distinctive set of moral qualities constituting its national essence, and (b) urge each individual member to make themselves the embodiment of national character.
>
> *Luciana Benincasa, Lecturer, University of Ioannina, Dept. of Philosophy, Education and Psychology, Section of Education, Dourouti, GR-45 110 Ioannina. E-mail: luciana@cc.uoi.gr*

Introduction

Images of the nation and national character are produced, reproduced and propagated in social interaction, both in everyday life and on "special days" such as national days. After discussing the romantic model of the nation and the concept of national character, the paper proceeds to a description and analysis of some aspects of the rhetoric of speeches that teachers give at school on national days, drawing specifically on examples from Greece. A view of the nation as a "natural unit" becomes the basis for the alleged "national character." This in turn leads to a particular reading of history where the concept of destiny has a major part. At the same time, though, heroic behaviour may succeed in altering that destiny, when it is felt as unjust.

Conceptual Framework

The Romantic Model of the Nation
Developed after the French revolution, the Romantic movement dominated European culture, especially in Germany, Britain and France, roughly until the revolutions of 1848. By the middle of the 19th century the ideas of German romantic nationalism had become widespread all over Europe. In what is considered the typical Romantic view, humankind consists of nations–natural solidarities, corresponding each to one people and one culture. Each of these concepts – nation, people and culture – refers to a whole in which the single individuals are not important in themselves but rather as instruments of the national destiny. The Romantic view of history revolves around the concept of nation (in Greek, *ethnos*).[1] For Herder history is the interplay of nations – rather than individuals – each of which represents an unchanging category of people and a unique side of humankind (Breuilly 1994; Dumont 1983/ 1988; Eleftheriadis 1999; Kiriakidou-Nestoros 1978).

Unlike the collectivities of liberal theory, which individuals join and leave according to wish and rational choice, membership in the organic being of nation is not chosen. One belongs to a nation as one belongs to a family, "by nature" (Herzfeld 1992; Hutchinson 1994; Smith 1995: 31). Nature, or what is viewed as such, is set as the highest moral order: whatever contributes to the preservation of that order is "good." Conquest is always disruption of natural development and, accordingly, resistance to conquest always marks the highest points in the "life" of a nation (Breuilly 1994). Each nation is endowed with a mission and a destiny. It is a teleological view of history not unlike the one that appears, though within different frames of reference, in Christian thinking, the Enlightenment and Marxist philosophy (Ferro 1981/2001). Teleology consists of "reading the appropriate trend into events" (Breuilly 1994, p. 109). It consists of attaching *meaning* to events. Depending on the standpoint one takes, one and the same event may have different meanings attached to it.

Metaphors of the Nation

Metaphors translate something indefinite into something more comprehensible, and the body, the self and the family are the most immediate signs available as vehicles for metaphor. The nation is often metaphorically represented as an organism, with a body, a heart and a soul (Thalassis 1993). Offering images that seem natural, these metaphors provide the foundation for claiming that the nation is a natural subdivision of humankind (Herzfeld 1992: 75–76).

Unlike membership in a state or a socio-economic class, membership in a nation, when perceived as grounded in common kinship and common ancestry, sustains the idea of continuity, i.e. sameness through time. The family metaphor has been very common and fairly productive, as testified e.g. in English by terms such *as fatherland, motherland* and *homeland*. If the discourse of the nation conflates biological and cultural essentialism, this is largely due to the family metaphor, inasmuch as, through the idea of race and common blood, culture comes to be seen as biological inheritance. Human beings frequently define kin groups in biological terms, and then attach "cultural" attributions to these biologically defined relationships; by extension, when the nation is defined using kinship metaphors, aspects of national character are phrased in terms of "natural" and "innate" attributes (Herzfeld 1992).

National Character

Acting within history, nations manifest their national spirit (*Volksgeist*). The concept of *Volk* and the related notions of national spirit and national character (Kiriakidou-Nestoros 1978), were first elaborated by the German humanists, and further developed by Herder and the German romanticists (Breuilly 1994). In this tradition nations, peoples and cultures tend to be viewed as organic beings endowed with certain qualities immanent in the group – physical qualities that are charged with a moral value (Herzfeld 1992). It is the view of the nation as an organism that makes the construct of national character "thinkable": like individuals, nations, as well as peoples and cultures, have a character – a unique character, an essence – that is as old as the nation itself and that remains unchanged through time. In this view, national character is not seen as the product of common life in the same place and common experiences. Rather, it is innate, given from above, "natural" to the individual or group (Dumont 1983/1988; Eleftheriadis 1999; Kiriakidou-Nestoros 1978).

Deviations from the original order of nature, e.g. from the natural character, are unnatural and therefore bad. They require return to the "natural" situation and to the "spirit of that past" (Breuilly 1994: 108). Character is said to be inherited, and therefore predictable. It is clear however that "inheritance" stands here for "retrospective reconstruction" (Herzfeld 1992: 137–139). The view of the nation as an organism with its own character brings with it the concept of national destiny. The set of characteristics traditionally attributed to the nation marks the boundaries of a moral community, becoming "the basis for action, or at least of after the fact justifications" (ibid.: 78).

Within the view of the nation as meaning it would be superfluous to ask whether national character really exists or not. Inasmuch as the idea of national character exists for people and affects their behaviour, then it is real as a social category.[2]

Production and Propagation of Ideas about National Character

National stereotypes present and oversimplify national character as something fixed and unambiguous. Whether or not people really conform to these stereotypical images in their private life, they make rhetorical use of the stereotypes and they "expend considerable effort in reproducing them" (Herzfeld 1992: 72). Ideas about national character are socially produced and socially propagated. Science has constituted an important channel of such production and propagation. In fact, intellectuals from disciplines as varied as philology, biology, ethnology, history, linguistics and anthropology have all contributed to "prove" that nations are "obvious and natural divisions of the human race" (Kedourie 1994: 53). Billig shows how discourse about national character and national stereotypes is produced, reproduced and propagated in everyday interaction (Billig 1995). Formal education makes its own contribution to this process, both through the teaching and learning activities of the official curriculum and through the informal learning situations of school rituals and celebrations.

Discourses about national character "are simultaneously descriptive and normative" (Neiburg & Goldman 1998: 69). Bourdieu's (1986/1991, 1992) concept of rite of institution[3] may be used to illustrate the normative aspect. The process of institution consists of a naturalization of properties of a *social* nature. The rite of institution contributes to this process inasmuch as it creates discontinuities out of the social continuum and "consecrates the difference," thereby legitimating an "arbitrary boundary." Due to the "social magic" brought about by the rite, social, economic and cultural boundaries come to be experienced as natural boundaries by the people involved (Bourdieu 1986/1991, 1992). We can view public ceremonies about the nation (or any instance of use of a national stereotype) as rites of institution in that they create (or re-create) discontinuities out of the continuum of humankind, "consecrate the difference" across human groups and legitimate the arbitrary boundaries between them. By taking part in rites of the nation, young group members are consistently exposed to the view that nations are the building blocks of humankind.

Behind every rite of institution the message is "Become what you are." The constraints that the rite imposes on the individual (Bourdieu 1992) are part of its normative character: "Behave like a Greek." Rituals of the nation discourage individual members from courses of action that do not correspond to the "national character" that is believed to be peculiar to their national group. On the other hand rituals encourage individuals to realize their own "nature" as members of the nation. Since behaving according to nature is "good," it would be morally condemnable for a Greek, for example, to fail to behave "like a Greek."

Romantic Nationalism in Greece

The idea of national identity, which had been cultivated by Greek intellectuals throughout the Ottoman period, was systematized and politicized during Greek Enlightenment, between the second half of the 17th century and the start of the revolution. The Romantic conception of history and national character was thus "*un herdérisme avant la lettre*," expression of an "indigenous Romanticism" that developed independently of European Romantic nationalism (Kiriakidou-Nestoros 1978). Widespread among the intellectuals, even the most progressive and radical promoters of Enlightenment ideas, this conception coexisted with views such as freedom from arbitrary power, anticlericalism, equality and in general with the liberal principles that had inspired the Greek revolution of 1821 and the first constitutions of the new state (Kitromilides 1990; Kokkonas 2000; Pizanias 2000).

Since then, and in spite of the postwar shift towards issues of social justice, political romanticism has been a feature of Greek political thought, both within the "traditional Right" and within the "populist Left" (Eleftheriadis 1999: 47). According to Dimaras, "Greece [is] one of the nations that ... may be characterized as Romantic *par excellence*" (Dimaras 1985: 473). The organic conception of the nation as a "transcendent holistic entity" that served the creation of the Greek state in the 19th century has fossilized, and Greek society remains attached to it, in spite of the fact that both society and historical knowledge have changed (Liakos 2001a, 2001b). Greek social scientists, politicians and people in the street alike describe the Greeks in terms of eternal and unchanging "characteristics of the race/ nation" (Paparizos 2000)[4].

The National Day Commemorations
In Greek schools there are two main national celebrations. One of them commemorates the start of the struggle for independence from the Ottoman Empire, conventionally dated 25 March 1821, which eventually led to the founding of the Greek nation-state. This is also the date of celebration of a major Christian religious festival – the Annunciation by the Archangel Gabriel to the Virgin Mary. The other major celebration relates to Mussolini's attempt in 1940 to occupy Greece as part of the expansionist campaign of the Axis Powers. At that time the Prime Minister of Greece was Ioannis Metaxas. On the night of 28 October 1940 the Italian ambassador delivered to Metaxas an ultimatum: as a guarantee that the Greek territory would not be used by foreign powers as the basis of war activities against Italy, the Greek government was asked to allow Italian troops to occupy strategic positions in Greece. The Greek government refused, and the people threw itself with enthusiasm in the struggle. This event and the battles which followed between Greek and Italian troops on the Albanian border, known in Greece as the "Albanian epos" (*Alvaniko epos*[5]), are commemorated every year on 28 October, a date and celebration known as "the No" (*to Okhi*). Some speakers, though not all, combine this occasion with remarks about the German-Italian occupation that followed in 1941, and with a celebration of the movement of National Resistance.

An acquaintance pointed out for me that there might appear to be problems for speakers on *Okhi* Day, which are not faced by speakers on 25 March. The War of Independence had a successful outcome inasmuch as it led to the foundation of an independent Greek state. But after October 1940, and the struggle of Greek troops, under appalling conditions in the winter of 1940/41, to force back the Italian troops, Germany invaded Greece in April 1941. Even if one wanted to ignore the long term result of the Greek Civil War, the 1940 campaign, in which the Greeks could not eventually prevent their land being occupied, would seem more a failure than a success. An outsider might conclude that there is not much to celebrate. Yet the celebration does make sense.

First, the speakers place emphasis on the short-term victories on the Albanian front and on the Greek soldiers' heroism in a struggle that from the very beginning showed so "unequal" (in most speakers' words). Furthermore, as Greek scholar Koulouri (2003) explains, "the decision of Greece to resist Italian and German fascism goes far beyond the defence of national independence and is associated with the defence of universal values, such as freedom and democracy" (Koulouri 2003: 78). According to two non-Greek scholars "the Greek victories had a wider significance than their modest military results. At a time when England alone faced Germany and Europe was prostrate, the Albanian campaign was the first defeat suffered by the Axis. The sympathy and admiration of the free world was consequently unstinted" (Campbell & Sherrard 1968: 171). These views are emphatically expressed in the speeches too.

Methodological Approach

The Research Questions
How are the celebrated events (revolution and resistance respectively) presented in the speeches? Why and how, according to the speakers, did the Greeks struggle? What for? And how, according to the narrator, did they manage to reach the results that are the object of the commemoration?

The Sample
The paper is based on a corpus of speeches that were not written for the purpose of contributing to this study. In this sense, I can claim that I adopt a nonreactive method (Brewer & Hunter 1989) inasmuch as I had no part in the production of the speeches, and the speechmakers were "unaware of being parties to research" (ibid.: 128).

The speeches examined in this paper, thirty-eight in number, have been collected in secondary schools in a provincial town in northern Greece between 1998 and 2003. I collected part of them at the end of the relevant school celebrations that I attended either as an outsider or as a teacher, by simply asking the speaker for a copy of the speech. Since commemorations are held at the same time in all schools, for each commemoration I could attend the relevant celebration in one school only. Therefore I asked acquaintances in the teaching profession to hand me their own speech after the celebration. This means that the data consists of written texts, or, better, of texts that were written for the purpose of being delivered in public.

Having attended these celebrations for several years, I have the impression that usually these speeches, rather than strictly individual creations, are individual enactments of a widely shared social memory—widely shared, in some general lines, at least for the purpose of celebrations. Though each speech has its own style and emphasis, whole (groups of) sentences can be met, in exactly the same form, in more than one speech. As to the status of these speeches, though they are materially written and delivered by individuals, only to some extent can they be considered individual products. Teachers often write their speeches with the help of history school textbooks. Alternatively, they may consult one or more of the several books of speeches commercially available. Moreover, teachers often borrow speeches from one another, sometimes adopting them as they are, more often cutting something and/or adding something else, or combining different speeches in various proportions. To some extent, individual preferences do come into the picture, and this is why most times each speech has a high degree of coherence. At the same time, though, because of what I said above, each speech may better be viewed as a collective creation.

It follows that details such as the gender of the speechmaker or the type of school a certain speech was delivered at are not relevant. Moreover, being interested in the language used rather than the people generating the language, I do not repute important to specify how schools or teachers were selected. It might be important, though, to mention the political situation at the time the speech was delivered. Actually, around 1974 there was an important shift in the way of dealing with the October commemoration (Koulouri 2000), but this issue, which has important implications for a particular aspect of the October speeches, is not within the scope of this paper. The socialist party was in power almost uninterruptedly from 1981 until May 2004 (with the exception of a four-year period between 1989 and 1993), and the political climate has not changed so as to lead us to expect a change in the type of speeches delivered in school.

The Analysis

I first grouped answers to the research questions in two categories that I called *in-order-to* and *because-of*. These terms were originally used by Schutz in the context of a theory about the motives for people's actions. Whereas because-of motives lie in past experience, in-order-to motives point to a future state of affairs that the actor wishes to bring about (Schutz 1971) In this paper, by the terms "because-of motives" and "in-order-to motives" I mean explanations/ justifications of actions, respectively (a) in terms of cultural features, feelings or beliefs, that, according to the speaker, made those actions necessary and possible, and (b) in terms of something the action was directed to bring about, i.e. goals and objectives.

Why these categories and not others? Because, after repeatedly reading the speeches, the two categories seemed to emerge from the material and produce an interesting reading key. After sorting the instances in the two categories above and re-reading the speeches, I noticed repeated terms, concepts and statements that suggested that the two categories could and should be combined again, and I found that this made sense from the standpoint of the Romantic paradigm.

More or less this is the way I dealt with the rest of the analysis. I read and re-read the speeches many times in a kind of continuous dialogue with the material. The categories of fate and destiny, for example, stood out at once. When I came across words/ phrases/ points of view that differed from the mainstream approach, I took note of them. These instances helped me see what the mainstream speeches did *not* say. In fact, absence is not less meaningful than presence (Bateson 1972).

A Few Words about Myself
Born in Italy, I moved to Greece in 1979 when I got married to a Greek citizen. I worked as a teacher in state schools in Greece from 1987 to 1992 and again from 1998 to 2000. Until then I had attended national day commemoration with some special interest, and sometimes I even felt moved to tears, but without planning to write any paper about that interesting aspect of school life yet. Since 2000 I have been a lecturer at a Greek university and I have started developing an academic interest in teachers' speeches.

The National Day Commemorations at School

On the two national days, shops and public services are closed. Commemorations are held in all schools, following the procedure stated in the relevant presidential decrees and circulars of the Ministry of Interior. In towns, celebrations in schools are held on the day before, whereas on the day of the commemoration school staff and students gather at a church in the school neighbourhood. There, during the liturgy, a teacher delivers a speech. After that, the army and the pupils parade in the centre of the town. Each school contributes to the parade with a group of students. The top student from each school parades carrying the national flag. Parades attract a great number of inhabitants – not just the parents of the pupils parading – who stand at the sides of the street, watch and applaud every now and then. From a platform set up for the occasion, representatives of the local political, military and religious authorities attend too, together with a delegate sent by the government.

At schools, commemorations are held in the celebration hall, when there is one, or just in the school hall, which usually is large enough to host the public. It is mostly pupils and teachers who attend, but sometimes parents attend too, especially at primary schools and especially on *Okhi* Day, when the commemoration includes the awarding of prizes to the pupils who had achieved the best grades at the end of the previous school year. A commemoration always starts with a speech, usually delivered by a teacher who reads out of a written copy. Usually the speechmaker is one of the teachers who teach Greek (ancient and modern) and history (*filologi*). One reason is that these teachers are expected to have, by definition, the necessary historical knowledge for writing a speech as well as for choosing the relevant poems and songs. Another reason is that these teachers are perceived as generally more skilled at writing. Sometimes, especially in upper-secondary schools, the speechmaker is an elder student, though even then the speech may have been written by (or with the help of) a teacher. A commemoration also includes songs, poems, readings from school anthologies or other texts. At the March commemoration one may also see one or more sketches that dramatize events related to the theme of the celebration. A commemoration always ends with the participants standing and singing the national anthem. A detailed description of these celebrations is provided by Bonidis (2004).

The Context
People who attend a school commemoration are aware that other people in other schools sing the same anthem on the same day, at more or less the same time, using the same language (Anderson 1991), and that this happens within the boundaries of that portion of the world called Greece. Moreover, the people gathered at a celebration may be aware that for decades in the same school, and in the very same ceremony hall, past generations of pupils and teachers have met for the same purpose, recalling the same events and concluding the rite with the same anthem.

As to the school context in which these speeches are embedded, recent studies show that textbooks, produced by the Ministry of Education and Religious Affairs, teach the pupils to think in rigid representations and national characteristics. On the whole Greek education has a strong ethnocentric character. The history taught at school, revolving around the idea of the nation as an eternal and natural essence, is to a large extent mythology. The basic categories of the discourse about the nation are continuity, preservation, resistance, homogeneity and superiority. Teaching is heavily based on the textbooks and little margin is left for teacher initiative (see individual chapters in Dragona & Frangoudaki 1996; see also Avdela, 1996a; Avdela 1998; Frangoudaki 2001). Interviews with teachers serving in primary schools with a high percentage of pupils from a non-Greek, non-Orthodox background show that those teachers believe that a fundamental part of their task is to preserve Greek heritage and shape the pupils' national consciousness (Inglessi 1996).

In-order-to ...
What did the Greeks struggle for? They struggled for preserving honour and dignity, for defending their "holy land," their glorious historical past and the ideals of the fatherland, which grant the nation's survival. They struggled for the liberation of the *ethnos*, for freedom, democracy, independence and peace. They fought against obscurantism, violence and subjugation. A few speeches, though not the majority, take into account – to a lower or higher degree – a social dimension to the struggle. Thus some speeches mention a "struggle with a social content against any oppression," though without further developing the analysis, while in one case a class approach constitutes the very backbone of the speech. To the above goals, most March speeches add the struggle for the "holy faith of Christ" and the attempt to "urge upon the whole of Europe the righteousness of our [the Greeks'] claims."

Attributing a universalistic dimension to the revolution, some speakers say that the struggle took place for "pure ideals and the basic values of the civilized world" that "were being threatened by crude and open violence." This theme is overwhelming in the October speeches.

Because-of ...
Why did the Greeks struggle? And why/how did they win? They struggled because they have a high sense of honour and deep love of the fatherland; because they have patriotism; because the flame of freedom has never quenched within the Greek struggler; because for the Greeks the struggle for freedom and democracy is a way of life. In addition to "the free Being of the Greeks" and their "hate for the enemy," March speeches place stronger emphasis on freedom, something – they state – that Greeks have never given up fighting for. They struggled and won because for the Greeks "freedom is a way of life"; because they have "struggleness"[6], because "Jesus Christ and Greece were vibrating – within the Greek soul and they did not let it accept the idea of subjugation." Next to the Greeks' "faith in God," which urged them to revolt, there sometimes appears another kind of faith that adds a universalistic dimension to the struggle. It is the faith in the "noblest human ideals," the "eternal moral values," and the "universal, panhuman claims for freedom, peace and dignity."

"History is the Mirror of our Character"
In both the March and the October speeches it is claimed that each people has a distinctive attitude towards life: "The history of a people is substantially the history of a few moments in which it confirms its will to either live actively, autonomously, and in accordance with its peculiar attitude to life or to die."

The struggle is explained by the "essence" that the Greeks "had carried within them for centuries." Their "noble deeds" are a demonstration of that essence, which consists of a number of distinctive marks. Also referred to as "gifts" and "virtues," these distinguishing features consist of "our values as a nation" and the "imperishable ideals of our race" (see Note 1 for the term "race"), but also include the "perennial bad sides of the race." In fact, in this model nations have not only innate gifts but also innate bad sides[7]. A speaker states: "History is the mirror of *our* character"[8] (Emphasis added). The following quote summarizes most of these values and ideals:

"With the struggle of 1940 all those distinctive values that define our Nation were brought out – the adoration and the infinite love of the Greeks for freedom – a freedom that, in Kazantzakis' words, is not "fall, pie, so that I can eat you." It's a fortress, and you conquer it with your sword." (...). The sense of dignity, the national[9] and individual sense of honour (*filotimo*), the sense of good and the strength of imagination are additional distinctive marks – jewels – of the Greek race."

Further "distinctive features" of the "race" are determination, courage, audacity, an indomitable soul, endurance, a strong sense of duty towards the fatherland, greatness, strength and "struggleness." One of the most quoted "national virtues" is "love of freedom," which is described as "created by the Greek race" (or "naturally Greek"; in the original, "*yennima thremma tis Ellinikis filis*"). The Greek nation "proves to be unique among all the peoples on the earth." Those unique characteristics, the "virtues of the race" constitute the nation's "compass" in her navigation through history. These moral qualities are "distinctive marks (...) of the Greek race, (...), of national and personal conscience." Thus when the Greeks carry out their duty as Greeks they feel proud: "And we are proud because we had been born Greeks and we had fought like Greeks." This unique set of characteristics is glossed as "our Being" or "Greek soul," "indomitable and proud," "perennial and imperishable," "created to live free and independent."

The continuity stressed in the speeches is not only material and biological, but cultural as well: "Not only did the Greek people manage not to die out and disappear, but kept its national consciousness unpolluted." The continuity is further stressed by suitable time words: the fatherland "never" surrenders, the Greek people's desire for freedom is an "everlasting yearning," their ideals are "eternal," and their "passions inspired by God" date back to the "very beginning" (the beginning of what is not specified), just as the Greek soul and Greece itself are immortal. Similarly, the word "our Being," which in Greek is expressed with the infinitive form of the verb (*to ine mas*), places the nation out of time. This Being, this soul, seems to contain its future in itself: "The Greek soul cannot possibly ever live in slavery. Greek blood is destined to flow in the veins of free human beings." In a school, a poster in the central corridor read: "Greek child, don't forget that you're a Greek, and within you shines indomitable the soul of the *yenos*" (see Note 1 for the term *yenos*).

Though one speech notes how during "centuries of slavery" the people gradually *developed* national consciousness, most speakers seem to subscribe to the theory of national awakening: after four centuries during which the ethnos was in "coercive hibernation," the "Teachers of the *Yenos* [early supporters of Greek independence, *N.o.A.*] managed to awaken and activate the latent national consciousness." The categories *nation*, *race* and *people* are not used with the same frequency in the two groups of speeches. In the October speeches the term *people* (Gr. *laos*) is the most common to refer to the in-group (almost seventy per cent of the occurrences). In a very few occurrences it is used in the sense of "the ones who do not have power in society." In all the others it means "Greek national body." The categories *nation* (Gr. *ethnos*) and *race* (Gr. *fili*) occur much more seldom but with roughly equal frequency (about fifteen per cent each). However, the particular context in which each term is embedded is often (though not always) different, as showed by the following examples: "And the struggle of our people (Gr. *laos*) against fascism started" vs. "the bowels of the *nation* quake."

In the March speeches the cultural category *ethnos* 'is the most common. The cultural category *yenos* is used too, but mostly, together with *race*, in those March speeches where the religious element is given prominence. The term is often capitalized and used without any qualifier, as in e.g. "the resurrection of the *Yenos*" (See note 1 for the capital initial of *Yenos*). *Race*, though, appears also in October speeches. *Hellenism* is occasionally used in both groups of speeches. There are individual variations across speeches as well. For example, some of them place greater emphasis on the concept of race. A few speeches refer to the categories that make up the nation e.g. town-dwellers, farmers, and so on, but usually only to stress the universal participation in the struggle, e.g. "all classes gave their blood and soul." In most speeches unity is simply taken for granted in the categories of *ethnos*, *yenos* and *race*. Some speeches explicitly stress it: "The creator of the 1821 Revolution is the whole *ethnos*."[10]

The emphasis on unity is consistent with the metaphor of the nation as a living organism, either a tree/ plant with "roots" and a "national trunk" or a body: the "nation-wide alert" makes "the bowels of the nation quake." Accordingly, nations are made the grammatical subject of verbs that are literally used for organisms: they "go into hibernation," and eventually "awaken"; they may die and resurrect, or be born again; finally, they may manifest their own "will". What is the place of each individual in the organism? One speaker states that "all of us constitute particles of a whole, and all of us are indispensable to the task of achieving the prosperity of this country."

The *ethnos*/ Greece (*Elladha*, feminine in Greek) takes sometimes the shape of a female body or of the most female part of a female body: a "uterus where the seed of freedom [has grown for centuries]." The boundaries of the territory of the nation are the boundaries of a female body: "A whole empire would rape our national boundaries in the most cruel way." The family metaphor (mother, children, brothers) and the blood metaphor are used, though not to a large extent.

Fate and Destiny
Especially in the March celebrations, speeches often mention fate and the "destiny[11] of the race." Through the centuries, the race has been "on a march along the road of its destiny," "as the fate of the race dictates." Fate has set out a written plan for all the peoples, and for each people separately: "And the peoples try to devoutly fall into line with their history and traditions as if out of a biological, organic need. For the Greeks this need is not only biological but national as well." Poems and songs, chosen by teachers and read by pupils during celebrations, reiterate these views. Sometimes complaints are voiced because Greece has got from fate less than she deserved: "The unjust fate of centuries (…) condemned the Greece of philosophy and democracy to endlessly embroil herself in wars and fights." According to one speaker, many times fate, jealous of Greece, opposes her plans.

The concepts of fate and destiny give one more answer to the question of why the Greeks struggled: "It's the destiny of the Greeks that their bones should crush and be blessed in struggles and sacrifices in which the only rewards are immortality and glory." The revolution is described as "the *fatal* outcome of the clash between just and unjust, between national pride and oppression and domination" (Emphasis added). The idea of destiny is echoed in phrases such as "the blessed time had come, the time of the proclamation of the revolution." The Greeks had lost neither courage nor hope, and "*in the fullness of time* their anger broke out" (Emphasis added).

The term "will" and related verbs are mentioned several times in relation to the Greek people. In the March speeches, the Greeks' "iron will" becomes "unbridled like the lion's will" because it is sustained by their love of freedom. The strong will of the Greek people, together with self-confidence and "struggleness," yearning for freedom, courage and strength "created in the Greeks the feeling that sooner or later their destiny must be changed." It is possible for a people to "change its historical course" and "escape from its unwanted destiny." Eventually the Greeks' struggle, conducted against all odds, does not leave fate indifferent:

"And the fate of Greece, which had kept her enslaved, regretted her own behaviour. And she [fate] ran to Mount Olympus and to Parnasus, to the Pindus and the Agrafa, to Mani and Souli and to other mountain tops, and suckled with her milk the heroes who fed the tree of freedom and brought about the resurrection of the fatherland".

The concepts of fate and destiny are used only in a few of the October speeches, usually to explain why the Greeks struggled: it is the destiny of the Greeks to have to face enemies, push back conquerors and always be present in great events.

Discussion

Circular Causality
How do the speakers explain action? How do they explain the start and conduct of the war of

liberation on the one hand, and the *No* and the "epos of Albania" on the other hand? The *why*, *how* and *what for* questions about the struggles can be answered with a double series of motives/ explanations: (a) the Greeks acted *in order to* achieve, among other things, freedom and independence; (b) they did so *because* they have always had a deep love of the fatherland, yearning for freedom and hate for tyranny. The *because-of* category includes several traits that are presented as unique features of Greek national character. An individual is born Greek, and from this simple biological reality springs behaviour. Culture is a consequence of biology: "We had been born Greeks and we had fought like Greeks." "Greekness" is an unchanging essence, the timelessness of which is stressed through the use of suitably chosen time words: "never," "always," "from the beginning" and "perennial" reinforce the stress on the continuity of the nation. That is, (a) the Greeks acted like that *in order to* achieve certain objectives, and (b) the Greeks acted like that *because* they are Greeks. Action is explained as both politics and meaning.

However, they had set those goals because they were/ are Greeks and so it was in their *nature* to set such goals. The actions performed by this people/ nation are the product of its national character, its essence and its nature: they fought *in order to* obtain freedom *because* it was in their nature to yearn for freedom. Ultimately, action as politics is reabsorbed into action as meaning. The example that best shows the circularity of the argument is maybe the statement that the Greeks fought, died, sacrificed themselves etc. because they have "struggleness"; that is, they struggled *because of* their "struggleness." Action is explained resorting to something contained in the performing organism rather than to a property of the interactive system of which the organism is part. This is not too dissimilar from what people do when they attribute e.g. an individual's act of aggression to their "aggressiveness."

An October speech states that "the *No* of that day was an act commensurate to all the noble deeds that witness to the unity and continuity of our race." First, who "we" are is used to explain what "we," i.e. our ancestors, did; second, our behaviour is judged consistent with the ancestors' behaviour and brought as a proof of the continuity of the race through what can be called a self-sustaining argument. Like all stereotypes, statements about national character are self-sustaining inasmuch as they resist regardless of disconfirming experiences. According to Daniel Goleman (1995), a self-sustaining way of thinking is one of the features of the emotional mind.

A Meaning in the Nation's History
Greece is perceived as having lost a great part of her past greatness. This constitutes a deviation from the natural order of things and must be corrected. It is "written" that Greece will recover her past glory and become great again if she recovers her past. When a teacher says that "the peoples who remember their history repeat it at higher levels, in superior spheres," he points to a process that consists at the same time of repetitions and progress. In this conception of progress the future depends on the past. The journey of the nation may be described as going back to the past in order to be able to go ahead into the future. It is like looking ahead to the past, or looking back to the future. It is said that "the peoples try to devoutly fall into line with their history and traditions (...)," as if a nation's history and tradition had an existence independent from the existence of the nation itself. It is as if a nation's history existed on a higher level of abstraction. This is reminiscent of Kroeber's conception of culture as "existing" in the area of the "super-organic," at an autonomous level of reality, independent from individual action and control (Cuche 1996/ 2001). The nation's "life" seems to be perceived as the attempt by each generation to imitate a super-organic model of the nation itself: "Let the destiny of the nation be our goal."

The march of the nation through time takes on a teleological character. In a teleological reading of events the past takes on meaning according to the way it is approached in the present and according to the kind of future that is perceived as desirable. It is as if the future influences the past and the present, producing a backward reading of events: it is the "magic of nationalism to turn chance into destiny"

(Anderson 1991: 10), or "to recast the contingent as the eternal and inevitable" (Herzfeld 1987: 84). Marxist philosophy and Christian thinking have viewed history as directed towards a goal that had been set as its end (Fr. *fin*, Gr. *telos*) and its completion. Both have seen a *meaning* in history: in the former case the meaning (Fr. *fin*) of the process is in the perfection of this world, in the latter case the meaning is somewhere outside this world (Le Goff 1986/1998: 173). From the standpoint of this nation, the meaning of history seems to be in the attainment of glories comparable to her past glories – that is, the re-establishment of the "natural" order. In one speech the final solution of the war of liberation is defined as the "the *fatal* outcome of the clash between just and unjust, between national pride and oppression and domination." This seems to point to a cosmology where not only everything is "written" from beforehand, but where Good always wins. History is the progressive realization/ triumph of Good. Since the nation is the incarnation of everything positive, Good is identified with the national group.

The Nation is an Organic Whole
The nation as a collective individual is the protagonist of history. Individuals are "particles in the whole," all of them "indispensable" for the "prosperity of this country" – a functionalist explanation in character with the organic metaphor. In most speeches the nation (*ethnos*) is a unit with a biological continuity, expressed in the concepts of *race* and *yenos*, and a cultural continuity consisting of national consciousness, values, ideals, and so on. Like an organism, the nation has within it from the "very beginning" all the information that will allow it to become what it is destined to become, though the question of the "beginning" is usually left in the mist. In fact, if one allows for the existence of some beginning of the nation, at the same time one recognizes its historicity, thus denying its necessity and its being part of the nature of things. This kind of cultural DNA reveals itself within the course of history. It is as if the future of a nation had *always* already been present (already written) within the nation itself.

In this view, talking about the future requires resorting to the notions of fate and destiny. Just as in the concept of race, biology is destiny, so in the concept of fate, culture is destiny (Herzfeld 1987; 1992). The concepts of fate and destiny are closely interwoven with the notion of national character as well. National character becomes destiny. Ritual is there to remind individuals of who they are and to confirm the classification that culture has imposed on the social world: "Greek child, don't forget that you're a Greek (...)." To what extent do the speeches really legitimate images of national character? The reply to this question is beyond the scope of this paper. However, some of the views about national character expressed in the speeches may be heard in everyday conversation. More than once, during informal conversations with young Greek people (mostly students), I have been told that the Greeks have certain characteristic features among which they usually mentioned love of freedom first. As to my remark that probably all peoples love freedom, usually they did not seem to see my point. It was as if they heard something out of their universe of meaning. Certainly *these* rites are likely to have the effect of confirming a certain social and moral order. At the same time, though, one should have in mind that (a) besides these commemorations and related speeches, other institutions act in the same direction, and (b) in the social sciences causality is not linear as in the natural sciences but rather circular (Bateson 1972): to the extent to which such rites really confirm and reproduce a certain social and moral order, they are also the *product* of such order.

"Fate Regretted Her Own Behaviour": The Nation Shapes its Own Destiny
In the statement "the peoples try to devoutly fall into line with their history and traditions (…)" it is as if peoples acted on the scene of the world as actors in a theatre, enacting a *script* that had been *written* long before they started acting and to the *writing* of which they have not contributed. The image of a *writing* fate is a feature of everyday discourse in Greece (Herzfeld 1992). However, the speaker states that the peoples "*try* to fall into line," implying that their "falling into line" is not automatic. Far from being puppets, individuals or peoples do have at

least some degree of agency. This is most evident in two speeches in which the role of fate becomes surprising: "The fate (*mira*) of Greece, which had kept her enslaved, regretted her own behaviour," eventually taking the side of the Greeks and helping them in their struggle. Initially hostile to Greece, fate feels compelled to change her mind because of the Greeks' heroic behaviour. This image does not match the image of the fatalist Greeks (or in general the fatalist Mediterraneans) that one can encounter in several ethnographies of the past. Fatalism, which means a "passive and total resignation to future events," has been attributed to Greeks by nations that have dominated them. Rather than being an indicator of fatalism, the invocation of fate – both in the speeches and in everyday speech in Greece – serves to rationalize damage *after* it has happened. Herzfeld (1992) points out the similarity between the resignation to fate usually attributed to oriental peoples and (Western) Calvinist notions of predestination. The "West" seems not to able to perceive the "other within the self."

Against charges of fatalism, several ethnographies of Greek villages show that struggle is a moral obligation and a leading concept in everyday life:

"anyone who does not do his best in this sense is unintelligent and deserves to lose the battle. Those who try may still fail, and then the villagers turn to fate or to God's will as an explanation. But an appeal to fate or to God is never an excuse for neglecting actions which are humanly possible" (Friedl 1962: 75).

Metaphors
Metaphors often point to a type of relationship among members of the nation that is natural and necessary. The metaphor of the body, for example, portrays the nation as an organism: "The body of Hellenism." The total sum of its members is often referred to as "the Greek" in the speeches. For certain purposes the body of the nation is a female body, for example in memories of past dangers or visions of possible future ones where conquest by foreigners is equated to rape[12]. Both the family metaphor and the body metaphor in some way convey the idea of continuity, which is a key idea in the textbooks, too. Any organism changes through time though remaining the same organism. As concerns the family, the idea of continuity is contained in the family name and, in some cultures, in the custom of naming children after their grandparents – a custom widespread in Greece. When infants are named after deceased relatives, new members come to replace the dead and this allows the family to take on a kind of immortality (Campbell 1964; Esposito 1989: 92–94).

Summary

A specific conception of the nation and history is propagated more or less consciously by secondary school teachers in Greece. The two national celebrations keep alive the memory of two important struggles in which the nation opposed foreign conquest. Since conquest is always disruption of natural development, resistance to conquest always marks the highest points in the "life" of a nation (Breuilly 1994). The struggles that are focus of the celebrations are presented as the natural result of a double series of motives: in-order-to motives and because-of motives. The in-order-to motives refer to goals that the members of the nation wanted to achieve, e.g. national freedom. The because-of motives refer to a set of distinctive traits immanent in the national group and as old as the group itself, that constituted the "natural resources" that made the celebrated action both necessary and possible. Given those national features, faced with the subjugation to the Ottoman Empire and Mussolini's invasion, the Greeks could only act as they acted: they revolted, fought and struggled because they are Greeks. Culture is used as an explanatory concept. The set of features, among which an immense love of freedom and a willingness to struggle are the most outstanding, amount to what within German Romantic thought is known as "national character." History, as one speaker states, "is the mirror of our character." The in-order-to motives are eventually re-absorbed into the because-of motives that constitute national character.

Given these presuppositions, history could

not have developed but the way it did develop. In a way, events were written from beforehand, and actually this idea is conveyed through the concepts of fate and destiny, repeatedly mentioned to explain the how and why of the main events. Fate is jealous of Greece and that is why she sometimes erects obstacles on the nation's path. However, on the basis of these speeches it is not possible to charge the Greeks of fatalism. This is apparent especially in two speeches where, faced with the courage displayed by the Greeks in their struggle and with their determination against all odds, fate regrets her behaviour and takes the side of the Greeks. That is, the Greeks *win* fate to their cause. Therefore, (national) destiny can be affected by behaviour.

Concluding Remarks

Speeches may be viewed as social texts: they do not simply reflect the social and natural world, but actively construct a version of the social and natural world. In this sense they have social and political implications. Through teachers' speeches, school rituals on national celebrations contribute to the production, reproduction and propagation of ideas about national character. Rites of the nation create discontinuities out of the continuum of nature and "consecrate" the resulting classifications imposed on the world. They "consecrate differences" and legitimate the "arbitrary boundary" (Bourdieu 1986/ 1991: 118) that divides the nation from other nations, thus confirming a model of the world according to which the continuum of humankind is composed of discrete, bounded and homogeneous nations.

Once the "arbitrary boundaries" around each nation are consecrated, the socially constructed order comes to be experienced as natural by the individual. Within this scheme nature (i.e. what is thought to be nature) is perceived as the highest moral order. The normative dimension of ritual is a consequence of the fact that the nation is felt to be part of the natural order. Like acts of institution, rituals of the nation invite each of the participants to become aware of the nature that they, as members of the national group, share with the other members, and to make their individual life the embodiment of national character.

Most of the speeches analysed in this paper present a model of the world as consisting of nations, with emphasis on the unity and homogeneity within each nation. Such an account proves problematic both as a model *of* and a model *for* society (Geertz 1973). As a model *of* society, like the models presented in textbooks, it gives an inexact picture of Greek society: besides concealing the existence of social differences and inequalities, it does not take into account the fact that people with a non-Greek, non-Orthodox background keep migrating to Greece. For the same reasons, as a model *for* society, the cultivation of the "nationalist mythology of the 19th century" (Frangoudaki 2001: R07) does not offer viable prospects for the integration of all these people who live within the boundaries of the Greek state and intend to stay. At school, celebrations that propagate such models of/ for the world are not easily conciliated with democratic demands for the integration of immigrants' children in Greek schools, which is a necessary step for their future integration as adults in Greek society. Maybe it is time to invent alternative ways of cultivating memory.

Notes

1. The historical knowledge produced today in the Greek academic and public discourse is based on the concepts of "nation" (*ethnos*) and "race" (*fili*) (Karakasidou 1994). *Ethnos* conveys both the concept of *ethnic group* and *nation* (Karakasidou 1993, in Triandafyllidou 1997, paragr. 4.2), *ethnicity* and *nation* (Herzfeld 1997: 78). Also, according to Tsatsos (as cited in Christopoulos & Tsitselikis 2003), in the Greek Constitution (art 1, par. 3) the term *ethnos* ("nation") seems to be related to the concept of *yenos*, in the sense of "race." *Fili* is used in the sense of "race" and also "people" (in a cultural sense). According to Herzfeld (1982: 133), it is a synonym for *ethnos*. The term *yenos*, which could be rendered as "lineage," is widely used by Church representatives in public speech. Vasiliou & Stamatakis (1992) define *yenos* as a blood-related group or the whole of individuals descending from the same first ancestor (*yenarchis*), forefather, and who constitute a group on the basis of particular social and religious rules. Zakythinos (1976) glosses *yenos* as "race," and Herzfeld (1992) defines

it as single, enormous kin group. It seems that there is some overlapping in the way these terms are used. As pointed out by Herzfeld (1987), the terms *ethnos, fili* and *yenos* all imply common descent.

Though until the fall of Constantinople reference had been made to the "*yenos* of the Greeks" and "our *yenos*," at some point in time the term started appearing without any qualifier, alone–the *yenos par excellence*. This has been interpreted as a sign that the idea of *yenos* had taken such proportions in "Greek consciousness" that adding any qualifier would only weaken its meaning: it was not any longer the *yenos* of the Greeks or "our *yenos*": it had become the *Yenos*, with a capital initial, and it came to be attached a strong moral content (Dimaras 1989; Kiriakidou-Nestoros 1978). Something comparable holds for the term *fili*, which in official Greek rhetoric is used without qualifiers to refer to the Greek people (*i fili*, or even *i Fili*, "the Race," with capital initial). As pointed out by Herzfeld, this usage testifies to the "absolute finitude" with which such ideas are articulated (1987: 214; 1997: 40).

2. For example, national frontiers, socially produced, "generate effects by acting on the self-perceptions of the communities they divide, and cause the formation, as time passes, of ways of being and feeling, ways of life and moral patterns" (Neiburg & Goldman 1998: 66).
3. Bourdieu (1992) proposes the term "rite of institution" as a substitute for "rite of transition." In this context, *institution* means *establishing in a position or office, investing*.
4. The following quotation is taken from the work of non-Greek scholars: "The legacy of Greece's unexpected resistance to the Italians was the confirmation of the personal and national virtues which some, especially foreigners, had begun to doubt any longer existed" (Campbell & Sherrard 1968: 173).
5. The transliteration of Greek terms and phrases (based on Herzfeld 1982, 1987) follows a modified phonemic system (real pronunciation).
6. Struggleness: In the original, *aghonistikotita*, from the word *aghonas*, which means "struggle". "Struggle" is a key word in the speeches, especially in the March ones. The war of liberation, which is the object of memory on March 25, is often referred to as simply "the Struggle," with a capital initial – like "the *Yenos*" and "the Race" (see Note 1). Therefore, I chose to make up a word such as "struggleness" rather than using e.g. "combativeness." Also "a love for struggle" seemed too weak, maybe because consisting of several words. Gregory Bateson narrates how the word "ethos", which he was using in fieldwork in New Guinea, revealed rather troublesome to work with, due to the fact that it is "too short." Thus, he tended to forget that he was dealing with an abstraction, and was handling the word as if it referred to something concrete and "causally active" in shaping native behaviour (Bateson 1972: 82). For similar (and at the same time opposite) reasons a phrase like "a love for struggle" would have been too weak in the context of this paper: I needed to express this emic term in *one* word only, so that it would sound as "causally active" as possible.
7. In the speeches the most quoted Greek bad side is discord (*dichonia*), which the textbooks condemn as harmful for the nation. The idealized image of homogeneity that emerges from the textbooks does not make pupils used to the idea that society hosts conflicting interests. Thus, instead of being presented as the normal condition, political struggle is morally condemned (Frangoudaki 1996a).
8. "*Our character*": The use of the pronoun "we" (us, our), meant to include all the Greeks of all times, can be called the "historically expanded we" (De Cillia, Reisigl & Wodak 1999).
9. Next to the adjective *ethnikos* (national), which refers to the political boundary (Cowan 1998), in the 1980s the adjective *ethnotikos* (ethnic) has come into use to refer to the cultural boundary (Angelopoulos 1997). The two adjectives derive from *ethnos* that conveys both the concepts of nation and ethnic group (see Note 1). A third adjective, the Greek *ethnik*, has lately appeared in phrases such as "ethnic music," "ethnic food" and "ethnic accessories," the last one used in the field of fashion.
10. Recent studies show that the textbooks used in Greek schools do not train pupils to distinguish between peoples and governments, or between citizens and political representatives (Frangoudaki 1996b, 2001). No reference is made to ethnic, cultural and religious differentiation within the national body, nor to social differences and conflicts (Avdela 1996b, 1998). As national homogeneity is a highest value and a necessary condition for group preservation, the image of homogeneity must be maintained. For the purpose of inclusion in history textbooks, the selection is operated so as to leave out events that could raise doubts about the image of unity and patriotism (Askouni 1996).
11. *Fate and destiny*: In the speeches three different words are used for concepts that belong to the semantic field of fate and destiny: *mira, peloponeso* and *imarmeni*. Mira refers to "the hypothetical and unexplainable force that is considered responsible for what happens to each human being." More specifically, it refers to (a) the personification of fate and (b) what fate has established for each human being. *Imarmeni*, which comes from the same root, means "the superior force that directs and influences the whole world, as well as the fortune of each human being." *Pepromeno* is the fate of each person. The

plural, *ta pepromena*, means "the mission and aspirations of a human group, as they have been shaped within the framework of historical development" (Idhrima 1998). In English the terms *fate* and *destiny* are often used as synonyms, but it is possible to draw a distinction between them. In this paper, following McArthur (1981), I use fate for "the (imaginary) cause beyond human control that decides events," and *destiny* in the sense of "that which must or has to happen." However, McArthur also suggests *fate* as a synonym of *destiny*. Due to the partial overlapping of the two terms in both languages, I have translated each occurrence with the English term that seemed in each case more suitable to the context, without trying to establish a fixed correspondence between a Greek and an English term. I do not refer to fate using the neuter form of the pronoun because fate is clearly personified in the speeches. I use a *feminine* pronoun because, since "fate" (*mira*) is feminine in Greek, this choice allows me to keep closer to the original, including the case in which fate is portrayed as suckling the heroes of the revolution.

12. In a comparative study of Greek and Turkish novels, the selected sample provided around 200 cases of inter-group romances or love stories between individuals belonging to the two communities. In almost all the cases the man is always "ours" (that is, Greek in Greek novels and Turk in Turkish novels) whereas the woman always belongs to the "other" category. According to the author, this is because women have traditionally been spoils of war: from a semiological standpoint, the husband is the winner in a strife (Millas 2001). I suggest considering the hypothesis that within the discourse of the nation, even when, like in love stories, the relationship between the partners is not antagonistic, the idea of boundary remains crucial. The boundaries of the territory of the nation are the boundaries of a female body. The woman's body is vulnerable, by nature exposed to "invasion": its boundaries are never safe. Though the love relationship does not take place within a conflict framework, in an inter-community love story each author probably unconsciously "chooses" to identify their group with the male partner, which may be taken as a sign that she or he is still on the defensive, in spite of all.

References

Anderson, Benedict 1991: *Imagined Communities: Reflections on the Origin and Spread of Nationalism*. London.

Angelopoulos, Yorgos 1997: Ethnotikes omadhes ke taftotites. I ori ke i ekseliksi tou periekhomenou tous [Ethnic groups and identities. The terms and the evolution of their content]. *Sinkhrona Themata*, 63, 18–25.

Askouni, Nelly 1996: Apenandi se dhio andithetikes fighoures tou "ethnikou allou": stikhia apo mia analisi tou loghou ton ekpedheftikon [Confronting two different images of the "national other": elements from an analysis of teacher discourse]. In: Thalia Dragona, & Anna Frangoudaki (eds.), *"Ti ine i patridha mas?" Ethnokendrismos stin ekpedhevsi*. Athens, Greece: 283–322.

Avdela, Effi 1996a: I singrotisi tis ethnikis taftotitas sto skholio: "Emis" ke i "alli" [The constitution of national identity at school: "We" and the "others"]. In: Thalia Dragona, & Anna Frangoudaki (eds.), *"Ti ine i patridha mas?" Ethnokendrismos stin ekpedhevsi*. Athens, Greece: 27–45.

Avdela, Effi 1996b: Khronos, istoria ke elliniki taftotita sto elliniko skholio" [Time, history and Greek identity within Greek school]. In: Thalia Dragona, & Anna Frangoudaki (eds.), *"Ti ine i patridha mas?" Ethnokendrismos stin ekpedhevsi*. Athens, Greece: 49–71.

Avdela, Effi 1998: *Istoria ke skholio* [History and school]. Athens, Greece.

Bateson, Gregory 1972: *Steps to an Ecology of Mind*. New York.

Billig, Michael 1995: *Banal Nationalism*. London.

Bonidis, Kiriakos (2004). Opsis ethnokendrismou sti skholiki zoi tis ellinikis ekpedhevsis: I ethnikes epetii tis 28 Okovriou ke tis 25 Martiou [Aspects of ethnocentrism in the school life of Greek education: The national commemorations of October 28 and March 25]. *Sinkhroni Ekpedhevsi*, 134, 69–84.

Bourdieu, Pierre 1986/1991: *Language and Symbolic Power*. Cambridge [G. Raymond & M. Adamson, Trans. Original work published 1986].

Bourdieu, Pierre 1992: Rites as acts of institution. In: John G. Peristiany, & Julian Pitt Rivers (eds.), *Honor and Grace in Anthropology*. Cambridge: 79–89.

Breuilly, John 1994: The sources of nationalist ideology. In: John Hutchinson & Anthony D. Smith (eds.), *Nationalism*. Oxford: 103–113.

Brewer, John, & Albert Hunter 1989: *Multimethod Research: A Synthesis of Styles*. London.

Campbell, John K. 1964: *Honour, Family and Patronage: A Study of Institutions and Moral Values in a Greek Mountain Community*. Oxford.

Campbell, John K., & Philip Sherrard 1968: *Modern Greece*. London.

Christopoulos Dimitris, & Konstantinos Tsitselikis 2003: Treatment of minorities and *homogeneis* [Aliens of Greek descent in Greece: Relics and challenges]. Administrative Secretariat of the Minority Groups Research Centre (KEMO). At <http://www.kemo.gr/archive/papers/ChristTsitse1.htm> Retrieved October 15, 2003.

Cowan, Jane 1998: Idiomata tou anikin. Poliglossikes (sin)arthrosis tis topikis taftotitas se mia elliniki komopoli tis Makedonias [Idioms of belonging. Multilingual articulation of local identity in a Greek town in Macedonia]. In: Dimitra Gefou-Madianou (ed.), *Anthropologiki theoria ke ethnographia. Sinkhrones tasis*. Athens, Greece: 583–618.

Cuche, Denys 2001: *I ennia tis koultouras stis kinonikes epistimes* [The concept of culture in the social sciences]. Athens, Greece [F. Siatitsas, Trans. Original work published 1996.

De Cillia, Rudolf, Martin Reisigl, & Ruth Wodak 1999: The discursive construction of national identities. *Discourse and Society, 10*(2), 149–173.

Dimaras, Konstandinos Th. 1985: *Ellinikos romandismos* [Greek Romanticism]. Athens, Greece.

Dimaras, Konstandinos Th. 1989: *Neoellinikos dhiafotismos* [Greek Enlightenment]. Fifth edition. Athens, Greece.

Dragona, Thalia, & Anna Frangoudaki (eds.)1996: *"Ti ine i patridha mas?" Ethnokendrismos stin ekpedhevsi*. Athens, Greece.

Dumont, Louis 1983/1988: *Dhokimia yia ton atomikismo* [Essays on individualism]. Athens, Greece [Original work published 1983].

Eleftheriadis, Pavlos 1999: Political Romanticism in modern Greece. *Journal of Modern Greek Studies, 17*(1), 41–61.

Esposito, Nicholas 1989: *Italian Family Structure*. Paris.

Ferro, Marc 1981/ 2001: *Pos afighounde tin istoria sta pedhia se olokliro ton kosmo* [How they narrate history to children all over the world]. Athens, Greece [P. Marketou, Trans. Original work published 1981].

Frangoudaki, Anna 1996a: I politikes sinepies tis anistorikis parousiasis tou ellinikou ethnous [The political consequences of the ahistorical presentation of the Greek ethnos]. In: Thalia Dragona & Anna Frangoudaki (eds.), *"Ti ine i patrida mas?" Ethnokendrismos stin ekpedhevsi*. Athens, Greece: 143–198.

Frangoudaki, Anna 1996b: "Apoghoni" Ellinon "apo ti mikinaiki epochi": I analisi ton enkhiridion istorias ["Descendants" of Greeks "since Mycenean times": Analysis of the history textbooks]. In: Thalia Dragona & Anna Frangoudaki (eds.), *"Ti ine i patridha mas?" Ethnokendrismos stin ekpedhevsi*. Athens, Greece: 344–400.

Frangoudaki, Anna (2001, November 17).'Iera iroika simvola ke meghales politikes andifasis [Holy heroic symbols and great political contradictions]. *Ta Nea*, p. R07.

Friedl, Ernestine (1962). *Vasilika: A Village in Modern Greece*. New York: Holt, Rinehart and Winston.

Geertz, Clifford 1973: *The Interpretation of Cultures*. London.

Goleman, Daniel 1995: *Emotional Intelligence*. New York.

Herzfeld, Michael 1982: *Ours Once More. Folklore, Ideology and the Making of Modern Greece*. Austin, TX.

Herzfeld, Michael 1987: *Anthropology Through the Looking Glass: Critical Ethnography in the Margins of Europe*. Cambridge.

Herzfeld, Michael 1992: *The Social Production of Indifference: Exploring the Symbolic Roots of Western Bureaucracy*. Chicago.

Herzfeld, Michael 1997: *Cultural Intimacy: Social Poetics in the Nation State*. London.

Hutchinson, John 1994: Cultural nationalism and moral regeneration. In: John Hutchinson & Anthony D. Smith (eds.), *Nationalism*. Oxford: 122–131.

Idhrima 1998: Idhrima Manoli Triandafillidhi [Manolis Triandafillidhis Foundation]. *Leksiko tis Kinis Neoellinikis* [Dictionary of Modern Greek]. Thessaloniki, Greece.

Inglessi, Chryssa 1996: "Na pame ksana se kapious dhromous ton pappoudhon mas, ton arkheon proghonon": O fovos ethnikis alliosis ke I ethniki aftoikona sto logho ton ekpedheftikon. Simberasmata merous ton pilotikon sinendevkseon ["Let's walk again on the roads of our grandfathers": The fear of national alteration and national self-image in teachers' discourse. Conclusions from a part of the pilot interviews]. In: Thalia Dragona & Anna Frangoudaki (eds.), *"Ti ine i patridha mas?" Ethnokendrismos stin ekpedhevsi*. Athens, Greece: 323–343.

Karakasidou, Anastasia 1993: Fellow travellers, separate roads: The KKE and the Macedonian Question. *East European Quarterly, 27*(4), 453–477.

Karakasidou, Anastasia 1994: Sacred Scholars, Profane Advocates: Intellectuals Molding National Consciousness in Greece. *Identities, 1*(1), 35–61.

Kedourie, Elie 1994: Nationalism and self-determination. In: John Hutchinson & Anthony D. Smith (eds.), *Nationalism*. Oxford: 49–54.

Kiriakidou-Nestoros, Alki 1978: *I theoria tis ellinikis laoghrafias: Kritiki analisi* [Theory of Greek folklore studies. A critical analysis]. Athens, Greece.

Kitromilides, Paschalis M. 1990: "Imagined Communities" and the Origins of the National Question in the Balkans. In: Martin Blinkhorn & Thanos Veremis (eds.), *Nationalism and Nationality*. Athens, Greece: 23–66. First published as a special issue of the *European History Quarterly*, 19: 131–134.

Kokkonas, Ioannis 2000, March 26: O ellinikos dhiafotismos ke o "loghos peri Eleftherias." *To Vima*, pp. 4–5.

Koulouri, Christina 2000, October 29: Afieroma. 60 khronia apo ton polemo tou ' 40. O Oktovrios ke o Ochtovris [Special edition. Sixty years after the war of 1940. October and October]. *To Vima*, pp. B3–B4.

Koulouri, Christina 2003, November 2: To ethnos yiortazi khoris na thimate [The nation celebrates without remembering]. *To Vima*, p. A 42.

LeGoff, Jacques 1998: *Istoria ke mnimi* [History and memory]. Athens, Greece: Nefeli [Y. Koumbourlis, Trans. Original work published 1986].

Liakos, Andonis 2001a, January 7: Apo ton lao sto ethnos [From the people to the nation]. *To Vima*, pp. B3–B4.

Liakos, Andonis 2001b, February 4: Eksinkhronizete i Istoria? [Does History modernize?]. *To Vima*, pp. 73.

McArthur, Tom 1981: *Longman Lexicon of Contemporary English*. Burnt Mill, Harlow, Essex, UK.

Millas, Iraklis 2001: *Ikones Ellinon ke Tourkon : Skholika vivlia, istorioghrafia, loghotekhnia ke ethnika stereotipa* [Images of Greeks and Turks. School textbooks, historiography, literature and national stereotypes]. Athens, Greece.

Neiburg, Federico & Marcio Goldman 1998: "Anthropology and politics in studies of national character." *Cultural Anthropology, 13*(1), 56–81.

Paparizos, Andonis 2000: I taftotita ton Ellinon. Tropi aftoprosdhiorismou ke i epidhrasi tis ellinikis orthodhoksias. In: Chrysoula Konstandopoulou, Laura Maratou, Dimitris Yermanos, & Theodoros Ikonomou (eds.), *"Emis" ke i "alli." Anafora stis tasis ke ta simvola*. Athens, Greece: 135–152.

Pizanias, Petros 2000, March 25: Aleksandros Mavrokordhatos: "Sas prosferoume dhiarki simmakhia" [Aleksandros Mavrokordatos: "We offer you a durable alliance"]. *To Vima,* p. 9.

Schutz, Alfred 1971: *Collected Papers*. The Hague.

Smith, Anthony D. 1995: *Nations and Nationalisms in a Global Era*. Cambridge.

Thalassis, Yorgos 1993: To soma ke to ethnos [The body and the nation]. *Dhiavazo, 322,* 73–76.

Triandafyllidou, Anna, Marina Calloni, & Andonis Mikrakis 1997: New Greek Nationalism. *Sociological Research Online* [Online], *2*(1), paragr. 4.2. At <http://www.socresonline.org.uk/socresonline/2/1/7.html#Karakasidou> Retrieved September 15, 2003.

Vasiliou, Thanasis A., & Nikiforos Stamatakis 1992: *Leksiko epistimon tou anthropou. Kinonioloyia, Ikonomia, Filosofia* [A Dictionary of the human sciences. Sociology, Economics, Philosophy]. Athens, Greece.

Zakythinos, Denis A. 1976: *The Making of Modern Greece. From Byzantium to Independence*. Oxford.

Between 'Föglö' and 'Fölisön'

Carl Björkman's Political/Performative Project of Autonomy c. 1880–1938 and the Location of the 'Finland-Swedish Nation'

Pia Maria Ahlbäck

Ahlbäck, Pia Maria 2004: Between 'Föglö' and 'Fölisön'. Carl Björkman's Political/Performative Project of Autonomy c. 1880–1938 and the Location of the 'Finland-Swedish Nation'. – Ethnologia Europaea 34:1: 61–70.

Through my deconstructive analysis of the individual case of the Swedish-speaking Finnish solicitor and joint leader of the Åland movement for reunion with Sweden, Carl Björkman, I show in this article that the phenomenon of Finland-Swedish nationalism (which began to gain firm ground in the late nineteenth century) was the challenged object of a supplementary national process with utopian characteristics from the very beginning. Björkman's personal negotiation of the central Finland-Swedish discursive constituents of coastal-cum-insular imagery led him to distance himself from Finland-Swedish nationalism and ultimately to be successfully engaged with the Åland movement for reunion with Sweden in the years 1917–1921. In its later inverted variety, however, Björkman's vision contributed to his own defeat in 1938, when he had to resign from his long-held position as the first *lantråd* of the autonomous islands. Björkman's personal national performance, with far-reaching political consequences, can nevertheless be said to have dislocated 'the Finland-Swedish nation' by strongly contributing to the – from a 'Finland-Swedish perspective – ironically tautological establishment of an autonomous Swedish-speaking community on Finnish territory. Since 1922, this community has had remarkably stronger legislative as well as symbolical means of action than the remaining Swedish-speaking population in Finland.

Pia Maria Ahlbäck, Dr. phil., Lecturer in Comparative Literature, Department of languages and culture, Åbo Akademi University, FIN-20500 Åbo. E-mail: pia.ahlback@abo.fi

Narrating nationalist ideologies as the performances of individual members of a nation is a way of negotiating the idea of the nation as chronologically and culturally coherent. This is one valuable result of Homi Bhabha's study on the discourse of nationalism "Dissemination: Time, Narrative and the Margins of the Modern Nation" (Bhabha 1994). Through the discovery of tropology as an effective means to analyse historiography, Hayden White has contributed the scholarly insight that national histories are made to appear in literary modes invested with particular subjectivities (White 1973, 1982, 1999).[1]

In this article, I shall discuss a number of Swedish past phenomena in Finland in the terms of post-colonialism and tropology.[2]

By introducing a few fragments of a particular Swedish-speaking world more than a hundred years old, I will place it in the critical discourse of nationalism. In that, I shall read the nearly forgotten leader of the so called Åland movement for reunion with Sweden,[3] the solicitor and politician Carl Björkman,[4] as *one* characteristically constitutive and yet atypical case of that phenomenon of nationalist ideology which in the beginning of the previous century came to be called 'Finland-Swedishness' (Sw. finlandssvenskhet, Fin. suomenruotsalaisuus).[5] Björkman's personal project of national performance can be seen to have challenged the Finland-Swedish nation in becoming by forming a supplementary national process eventually resulting in the autonomous Åland islands.[6]

The 'Finland-Swedish' 1890s: Supplementing a Nation in Becoming

At the open-air museum of *Fölisön* (Fin. Seurasaari) in the Finnish capital, eighty-five old buildings have been preserved, considered to have been particularly representative of the cultural landscapes in the various rural provinces of Finland between the 18th and the 20th century.[7] One of the museum buildings is the 18th century manor of *Kahiluoto*, which was moved to Fölisön from its orginal surroundings of *Töfsala* (Fin. Taivassalo) at the southwestern coast of Finland. In this manor Carl Björkman's family spent their summers during the second half of the 19th century.[8] The Fölisön Open-Air Museum was founded in 1909 by which time Finnish nationalism had flourished for some sixty years. By 1909 Swedish nationalism in Finland was reaching the point of its full self-awareness, i.e. the point of time when the coinage of the very concept of 'Finland-Swedishness' was made and entered the nationalist discourses. Accordingly, Swedish national sentiment in Finland had been looming well before that.

Walking into the manor of Kahiluoto we step into Carl Björkman's early world. The interior of the present day museal manor, however, has little to do with the original.[9] What was also – unknowingly – lost to the new owner, the National Board of Antiquities, was a document which would have added yet another thrilling layer of meaning to the manor had it been possible to preserve it in the reconstructed building at Fölisön. Upon his departure from Kahiluoto for *Åbo* (Fin. Turku) in August 1892, the nineteen-year-old student Carl Björkman wrote a poem in ten stanzas into the so-called book of Kahiluoto which his younger sister Gerda Maria had made by hand (Isaksson 1988). The motif of the poem was the dwarfed pine-tree with its gnarled branches. What is striking about Carl Björkman's poem is not only the fact that this was the one piece of poetry he ever wrote, or the fundamentally important fact that the poem cut right into that tradition laden with Swedish nationalist sentiment first appearing in the 1860s with this very tree at its core; a tradition which came to persist until 1946 (Zilliacus 1991, 2000). Crucial in this context is Björkman's variation of the motif. In at least one of the stanzas, the dwarfed pine with its gnarled branches on the cliff in its marine Western locale is returned as a thrillingly *ambiguous* metonym of the Finland-Swedish nation in becoming.[10]

Later on in this article I shall answer the question as to how, tropologically speaking, Carl Björkman's relation to the category of 'Swedishness' could be defined. Suffice it here to say that the well-known element of noble suffering inherent in the image of the marginalised but ancient Swedish-speaking (superior) servants of Finland is important. Nevertheless, this is not the most important aspect of the stanza. The idea of 'outpost' is indeed stressed; Björkman actually uses that very word, but there is a crucial twist in his use of the notion of 'outpost'. The dwarfed pine is constructed as the lonely 'outpost of the forest' on its cliff. The dwarfed pine with its threateningly gnarled branches points both backwards and forwards, inwards and outwards: to the Finnish inland and away from it; to a different, as yet unknown, place. The one thing impossible for the metonymic 'Finland-Swedes' of Björkman's poem is to remain in this condition of marginalization as it is connected with an immanent death. In Carl Björkman's poem, the branches of the pine-tree are gnarled in a threatening way due to its reinforced lack of community.[11] The poem accordingly gets the character of breaking point, point of departure and farewell. The dwarfed pine thus becomes not only threatened but *threatening*, to 'itself'. That is if it remains and persists in its condition of 'gnarliness', isolation. In other words, the achievement of Carl Björkman's vision is the very rupture in the nationalist imagery – threatened/threatening, marginalised/marginalising – and of the Finland-Swedish self-image in the making. It could be said that by perceiving the image of the dwarfed pine as expressing a threat to the *'itself'* of a Finland-Swedish nation in becoming – a nation that found its symbolical expression through that tree – Carl Björkman was highly sensitive to the Finland-Swedish nation's need for imaginary nourishment; the soft embrace of cultural and linguistic community.

In his discussion of the modern nation, Homi Bhabha points out that "the nation fills the void left in the uprooting of communities and kin, and turns that loss into the language of metaphor." Bhabha (1984: 139). The metonym of the dwarfed pine can be translated into kiplingesque imagery: here we find the white man's burden as a Scandinavian construct, the educated, upper middle-class, Swedish-speaking *man's* burden as the guarantor of Westernness in Finland.[12] The Finland-Swedish educated, upper middle-class discovery of the 'common' Swedish-speaking people and its oftentimes coastal and insular locations in Finland as an ideological property serves to form a Finland-Swedish nationalist "pedagogy", in Bhabha's words. He finds the construction of the nation since the mid-19th century to be ambivalently vacillating between the discourse of pedagogy and the discourse of the "performative", between the two of which a shadow would appear (Bhabha 1994: 145).

"The pedagogical founds its narrative authority in a tradition of the people (...) as a moment of becoming designated by *itself*, encapsulated in a succession of historical moments that represents an eternity produced by self-generation. The performative intervenes in the sovereignty of the nation's *self-generation* by casting a shadow *between* the people as 'image' and its signification as a differentiating sign of Self, distinct from the Other of the Outside" (Bhabha 1994: 147–148).

By placing the image of the dwarfed pine-tree at the centre of the Finland-Swedish nationalist discourse it becomes possible to witness in this metonym the bhabhaian 'split' of the nation into the poles of pedagogy and the performative, the 'shadow' growing in between them.[13] This is a process which could be seen taking place already in the late 19th century. At this time a Finland-Swedish ideology was beginning to be firmly established among other things through those narratives of past greatness when Finland belonged to Sweden, and through the exhortations for Swedish unity in Finland, both of which were mediated by the Finland-Swedish schoolteachers.[14] Simultaneously, however, at least one more kind of thinking and feeling about Swedishness in Finland was beginning to appear. This meant that those both far- and wide-reaching political activities which were to produce their final results in 1921 were beginning to be initiated. 1892 was the year when Carl Björkman started to imagine and document a different variety of 'Finland-Swedishness'. In having made its author "break with the environment into which he was born", as Carl Björkman himself once expressed his radical step of moving to Åland in 1902 and there becoming the leader of the movement for reunion with Sweden fourteen years later, the poetic fragment highlights the split between the national pedagogy and the national performative (Isaksson 1988: 30).

"We then have a contested conceptual territory where the nation's people must be thought in double-time; the people are the historical 'objects' of a nationalist pedagogy, giving the discourse an authority that is based on the pre-given or constituted historical origin *in the past;* the people are also the 'subjects' of a process of signification that must erase any prior or originary presence of the nation-people to demonstrate the prodigious, living principles of the people as contemporaneity: as that sign of the *present* through which national life is redeemed and iterated as a reproductive process" (Bhabha 1994: 145).

Carl Björkman's poetry writing and his move to Åland were two sides of the same coin, constituting a utopian act in a quest for cultural community and linguistic unity. This was a quest for the people-as-one-in and at-one-with its space and a different negotiation of the image of the dwarfed pine-tree with its, in Carl Björkman's view, threatening gnarled branches. What is central about the image of threat here is that the Finland-Swedish self-image was thus not constituted simply in terms of *noble* loneliness, hardness and endurance, but also in terms of *dangerous* hardness and endurance, of an immanent or foreboding death in the life of the nation and its people. Consequently: Carl Björkman's political manifestation of enacted utopianism at the individual level, as the necessary step in a process of personal autonomy which was to be constitutive in the production of political autonomy for a particular insular population later on, also helped to open up the national 'split'. By acting out the hope for the nowhere of the somewhere else in a radically concrete way, Björkman could be said to have been writing a "supplement" to the Finland-Swedish nation at a very early stage of that nation's existence.

In Bhabha's words:

"Once the liminality of the nation-space is established, and its signifying difference is turned from the boundary 'outside' to its finitude 'within', the threat of cultural difference is no longer a problem of 'other' people. It becomes a question of otherness of the people-as-one" (Bhabha 1994: 150).

What was later – in 1922 – to become the autonomous Åland islands was produced as *the* supplement to the Finland-Swedish nation, the autonomous province of Åland continuously thereafter at least implicitly insisting on being the 'proper' nation of Swedish-speakers in Finland.[15]

Tropes of 'Swedishness' in Finland

What remained of the Swedish-speaking nation in Finland thereafter can be said to have been no more than the genres of national tales as expressions of tropologically analysable modalities of 'Swedishness'. Bhabha states that "such an apprehension of the 'double and split' time of national representation" that he has proposed, "leads us to question the homogeneous and horizontal view associated with the nation's imagined community" (Bhabha 1994: 144). In her article "Hayden White: The Form of the Content" (Partner 1998), Nancy Partner takes White's ideas of historiographical texts as structured through tropes thus giving rise to narratives governed by literary genres into Bhabha's postcolonial world by means of the following statement: "In a rather abstract way, the culture wars, as played out between multicultural narratives of identity politics and national narratives of civic identity, are narrative wars" (Partner 1998: 171).

A return to Fölisön to rediscover Carl Björkman's poetic fragment, which by now has been *imagined into* the manor of Kahiluoto by means of this article,[16] will contribute to the understanding of Carl Björkman's project as productive of a certain variety of 'Swedishness' in Finland. The manor of Kahiluoto is a space belonging in the discourse of the 'lost Swedish earth' in Finland at the beginning of the 20th century.[17] Kahiluoto in its post-1920s museal location of Fölisön is a dystopian image, housing, however, the utopian potential in shape of the poem. Carl Björkman's poetic fragment does underline the image of a centered 'tragic' in Finland-Swedish history, but the poem read together with his future biography strongly enough expresses his project of autonomy which appeared to have taken the shape of an outright desire for the pastoral in a seemingly regressive move for many years.[18] The former family estate at Fölisön therefore manifests the end of an age whereas the poem indicates the contested space of Finland-Swedishness in becoming but also points beyond that space into a new order of national time. What can, consequently, be concluded about Carl Björkman's relation to the category of 'Swedishness'?

By leaving for Åland for good in 1902, Björkman opted fully for the pastoral. At the same time he turned down the tragic heroicism of the Finland-Swedish pedagogical narrative. His move would contribute to producing the future Finland-Swedish ideology as pale pastiche locked by a negative pedagogy. As such this ideology would appear to be wanting in national vitality due to its negotiation of the category of 'Swedishness' in terms of synechdochic runebergianism, an ideology constructed over an image in which the male Swedish-speaking and Swedish-writing authors of an idealised past Finland under Swedish sovereignty were central constituents. Moreover, also the reductive coastal spatiality of the new Finland-Swedish ideology could have been perceived to suffer from the same disease in that semiotic quest for 'Swedishness' where there always seemed to be something even more 'Swedish' to the west. Here I propose that the image of the sea became essential for the different qualities which the expression of the category of 'Swedishness' in Finland took. The image of the waves of the sea having touched no previous insular or coastal locations before reaching those of the Åland archipelago (or the other way round: Åland was always in the way so to speak) was necessarily powerful within such an imaginary loaded with national narcissistic desire. This particular logic of 'Swedish' imagery can be explicitly witnessed in the biography of Julius Sundblom.[19] Such connective imagery indicated a particularly intimate relationship. The name of 'Åland' became the sign of a privileged presence: that of Sweden. Björkman thus opted for a metonymic 'Swedishness' in which Åland became the name (nearly) substituted for Sweden itself, the imagined affluent part characterised by the spatial unity of language and culture – representing the absent 'Same' of Sweden. Carl Björkman, in other words, claimed what had been constructed as a more unmediated access to the exclusive/inclusive space of 'Swedishness', whose front page, back and centrefold undeniably were occupied by the former 'mother country' of Sweden. The Åland islands suggested a different order of time. The struggle between the national 'performative' and the national 'pedagogy' had not yet entered the scene and things remained like that up until about 1917, when the movement for reunion with Sweden was a fact. The life of the islands had been pre-modern or, expressing it tropologically, pre-generic. Up until this breaking point there had been one voice – that of the epic. One text in which the historical point of transition from unspoken, unimagined and pre-generic 'natural' space to spoken, imagined and generic national space can be concluded to have been marked was the fisherman Erik Karlsson's sentimental poem "Reunion".[20] The poem was recited at a reception in Stockholm in 1918 which was hosted by the Swedish king in honour of a delegation led by Björkman. The delegation presented the Swedes with an address which had been signed by an overwhelming majority of Ålanders expressing their intense wish to be reunited with the old 'mother country.' The well-known image of intimacy between Åland and Sweden was stressed: the Åland islands of the war in 1808–09 are pictured as "the baby being torn away from its mother's arm". The poem drew a full regressive circle. However, the outcome of the mentalities and events which it voiced was to be much more than so.

Carl Björkman himself accordingly became the one to perform the intervention, or to intervene by means of that performance, first as foregrounded fighter for reunion, and then in his capacity as *lantråd* from 1922 up until 1938. He became a firm defender of the Åland act of autonomy and took a persistently opposing, not to say hostile, attitude to the Finnish state. But what is more important: in that, as the performer of the autonomy which nearly granted Åland the profile of one more independent Swedish nation, Björkman gave in to the old heroic vision with tragic overtones. In 1938, the contours of a well-known image could be perceived in Björkman's new national pedagogy. The martyred dwarfed pine-tree of the Finland-Swedish coast had persisted after all – or returned. Facing the increasing threat of war, Björkman now wanted the demilitarised Åland islands armed.[21] The tragic, solitary load of the Finland-Swedish pedagogical national narrative turned up in Carl Björkman's new environment in the shape of a serious mis-reading on his part. But the lessons of this new, post-1922 national story were nothing like tragedy; they were rather comic and carnivalesque with strong spots of georgics in between. And he should have known: in Åland a mighty mass of dwarfed pine trees shared their own abundant space, as it were, with wooded meadows containing more varieties of flora than any place in Finland. In a way, Carl Björkman thus became the victim of that symbolical archipelago which he himself had known so well as to make it doubly supplement the Finland-Swedish national narrative.

These events find their appropriate comment in Homi Bhabha:

"The recurrent metaphor of landscape as the inscape of national identity emphasizes the quality of light, the question of social visibility, the power of the eye to naturalize the rhetoric of national affiliation and its forms of collective expression. There is, however, always the distracting presence of another temporality that disturbs the contemporaneity of the national present (...)" (Bhabha 1994: 143).

Through my investigation of the case of Carl Björkman by means of Homi Bhabha's postcolonial deconstruction of the modern nation and Hayden White's tropological analysis of nationalist historiography, I have shown in this article that what has been recognized as a 'Finland-Swedish nation' was a highly contested phenomenon already at an early stage of its history. Whereas Carl Björkman's early biography can be considered a perfect case study out of the Finland-Swedish nationalist pedagogy, his personal national performance must be seen as exceptional in the Finland-Swedish perspective. The particular example of nationalist ideology which Carl Björkman posed can be understood to constitute a utopian strand within the Finland-Swedish discourse of 19th and 20th century spatial marginality. This strand became instrumental to the production of the autonomy of the Åland islands and the political practices of its earlier years. Through that process, however, 'the Finland-Swedish nation' became neither extended nor strengthened, but subverted and supplemented by another Swedish-speaking 'nation' which governed itself on Finnish territory.

In the 1980s the 'Finland-Swedish' publishing company Schildts published a three-volume encyclopaedia with the title of *Finland*.[22] In that work Carl Björkman's dystopian and utopian national spaces – 'Fölisön' and 'Föglö' – can be found together; after one another, in the columns next to each other. Bearing Homi Bhabha's words in mind, this seems to be the appropriate space where to finally locate the historical phenomenon of 'the Finland-Swedish nation': between the columns of an encyclopaedia of *Finland* published in the Swedish language.

Notes

1. Whereas *Metahistory. The Historical Imagination in Nineteenth-Century Europe* (1973) might be White's most influential work, his two latest books *The Content of the Form: Narrative Discourse and Historical Representation* (1982) and *Figural Realism. Studies in the Mimesis Effect* (1999) have been the more important to my understanding of the historical phenomenon of Swedishness in Finland during the previous century.
2. The debates on which forms the expressions of the category of 'Swedishness' in Finland should, are allowed to or must not take are still in 2003 highly laden with ideological and dramatic sentiment. The choice of postcolonialism as my theoretical platform here is a deliberate attempt to distance myself from those debates and thus provide a radically widened perspective on such phenomena. A tropological reflection on the modalities of the category of 'Swedishness' since the 19th century and the age of nationalism seems more than motivated as that category continues to appear as a complex web of parts and wholes in varying degrees and constellations.
3. An extensive and detailed account in English of the far-reaching political effects internationally that this movement had throughout its existence is James Barros's *The Aland Island Question: Its Settlement by the League of Nations* (1968).
4. Who was Carl Werner Björkman? Carl Björkman was born into an educated Swedish-speaking upper middle-class family in the oldest city and former capital of Finland, Åbo (Fin. *Turku*), in 1873. Both Carl Björkman's father Werner Björkman and his uncle Herman Ithimaeus were solicitors and occupied central positions at the High Court in Åbo. His maternal grandmother Sofia Margareta Ithimaeus, née von Lode, was of Baltic-German noble ancestry and the owner of several large estates and manors in the southwest of Finland. Among those manors was that of Kahiluoto, inherited by Carl Björkman's mother Aina Björkman. The manor became the summer residence of the Björkman family for the latter half of the 19th century and the earliest years of the twentieth. Carl Björkman studied law at the University of Helsinki and graduated in 1902. Instead of following in the steps of his many prominent relatives he did the unexpected. Moving to the little municipality of Föglö in the Åland archipelago where he would live for ten years after which he was appointed mayor of the capital of the islands, Mariehamn, he became together with Julius Sundblom the primary leader of the Åland movement for reunion with Sweden in 1917–21. After the conflict had been resolved by the League of Nations in 1921, stating that the demilitarised Åland islands were to belong to Finland, the islands were granted a far-reaching autonomy and Carl Björkman was elected the first *lantråd*, i.e. chairman of the provincial government in 1922. This position he held until 1938, when he did not gain the support of the parliament of the islands, the *landsting*, any longer. He died in 1948 in the Åland islands. Before that, he had become *persona non grata* in the political life of the autonomous province despite his achievements for the islands and his

consistently radical defense of the autonomy. An enduring and gradually worsening conflict with his companion from the days of the movement for reunion with Sweden, the influential speaker of the *landsting* Julius Sundblom and his circle, contributed to Björkman's defeat. In 1936, Björkman became subject to attempted murder in his home due to this conflict. The single existing work on Björkman is Martin Isaksson's biography *Carl Björkman – Ålands första lantråd*, published in 1988.

5. In that, I shall (dis)place myself within the ambivalent home (lessness) of the English language, the *lingua franca* which provides me with a position from where to look at 'my own' space from the 'outside'.

6. The Åland movement for reunion with Sweden had a dual leadership. (See also note 4). The editor, school-teacher and native Åland islander Julius Sundblom was the other leader. In practice, however, Björkman's role was decidedly more active than Sundblom's during the *initial* years of the history of what in 1921 would become the autonomous Åland islands. This was partly due to Sundblom's obvious reluctance to accepting any visible role in the movement until the mid-phases of its four-year-existence. Sundblom, nevertheless, was one of the three representatives of the islands speaking for reunion with Sweden at the League of Nations Headquarters in Geneva before the League made the decision which granted the islands autonomy. Julius Sundblom was subsequently to become the most influential politician and celebrated public character of the autonomous islands, helped therein by his position as owner and editor-in-chief of the only newspaper in the islands, *The Åland*. Johannes Salminen's biography *Ålandskungen* (1979) is the one full-length study on Sundblom. I wish to emphasize that the aim of this article is not to take a stand on the truth value of the previous research in the field of the various aspects of the history of the autonomy (where Martin Isaksson's and Salminen's biographies on Björkman and Sundblom respectively are centrally included), but rather to open up that discussion for a discursively analytical approach. My reason for focussing on Björkman here is dual: his case is dramatically and problematically relevant to the very idea of *Finland-Swedishness*. Björkman's primary cultural context became influential for the processes eventually resulting in the autonomy but also for his own defeat. Accordingly, the historiographical category to which this article belongs is primarily that of mentalities, emotions and psychology.

7. http://www.nba.fi/MUSEUMS/SEURAS/Seurseng.htm 22.4.2003.

8. At the time when the manor of Kahiluoto was donated to the open-air museum of Fölisön in 1926 it had not been in the possession of the Björkman family for some twenty years. After the death of Carl Björkman's father Werner Björkman in 1893, the family's seven-room flat in Åbo was sold whereafter Aina Björkman moved to the Finnish capital with her children. There she had constant, occasionally severe, economic problems as well as problems with housing. She had ultimately to rely on economic assistance from her brother Herman Ithimaeus, vice-president at the High Court in Åbo and the owner of the manor of Tenhola in *Lemo* (Fin. Lemu) on the west coast which was not far from the island of Töfsala.

9. The 'museum' is one of those spaces in Western civilization which Foucault defines as heterotopias or 'other spaces' (Foucault: 1985–86; 1986). Foucault's essay on heterotopias was first published as "Des Espaces Autres" in the French journal *Architecture-Mouvement-Continuité* in 1984. The heterotopia reinvents the order between itself and the social space 'outside' of it. Heterotopias thus invert orders of perception. There are at least two English translations of Foucault's article – "Other Spaces: The Principles of Heterotopia" (1985–86) and "Of Other Spaces" (1986). When compared, these translations of the French original contain some important variations, among other things in the use of the attributes "different" and "other".

10. The stanza in question goes as follows in Swedish: "En tall med glesa och hotfullt vridna, / förkrympta grenar / på branten står. / En skogens utpost på enslig klippa" (Isaksson: 1988: 27). (A pine-tree with sparse and threateningly twisted, / dwarfed branches / is standing on the precipice. / An outpost of the forest on a solitary cliff. My transl.)

11. This is the well-known literary *topos* of Swedish 'solitude' in Finland after the rise of Finnish nationalism and russification. This topos, which is intimately connected to that of coastal and maritime symbolism, has attracted the interest of Finland-Swedish literary historians, critics, scholars and writers since its earliest days and continued to do so throughout the previous century. For a seminal reading of the topos as formative of a Finland-Swedish male prose tradition, see Mazzarella, Merete: 1989. *Det trånga rummet*.

12. Whereas the East-West dichotomy can be said to have been blindingly strong in Finland and partly continues to be so, phenomena such as Finnish and Swedish nationalisms as well as questions of identities and subjectivities do not yet seem to have been discussed in the terms of orientalism and postcolonialism to any extent or at all within the academy. Such a discussion would indeed be motivated as the Finnish strong need to continuously prove its status as a country of the 'West' stands in direct proportion to the cemented, twentieth-century-image of Finland *in* that 'West'

as either a part of the 'East' or as 'exotically' 'bordering' on the 'East'. The discourse of the-image-of-Finland-abroad which circulated in the Finnish media throughout the second half of the previous century mediated an overwhelming national anxiety as to the inverted ideological imagery of the desired 'Same' of the 'West'.
13. I am grateful to Robert Crawshaw for his suggestions as to the status of Bhabha's notion of the 'national performative' at the conference 'Literature and Its Others' in Åbo, May, 2003.
14. Johan Ludvig Runeberg's *Fänrik Ståls Sägner* (Eng. *The Tales of Ensign Stål*) and Zachris Topelius's *Fältskärns Berättelser* were central to this pedagogy. Despite the fact that Runeberg and Topelius were Swedish-speakers and wrote in Swedish they were not 'Finland-Swedes'. This ideology is a phenomenon of a later date. Runeberg's and Topelius's most popular works were also concerned with the whole country of Finland. However, these works told the tales of an idealised time when Finland was still a part of Sweden and, in the case of Runeberg's *Fänrik Ståls Sägner*, topicalised the tragic heroicism of the Finnish army in the war of 1808-09 when Sweden had to cede Finland to Russia. There was, accordingly, a shared quality of 'Swedishness' – which needed to be emphasized – between the Finland-Swedes in becoming and the earlier great national writers, their language, works, and ideology. Runeberg and Topelius could therefore well contribute to serving the purpose of constructing the self-image of a nation of Swedish-speakers in Finland. In other words, there is a synecdochic relationship between Finland-Swedish nationalism and the pre-Finland-Swedish, Swedish-speaking, Finnish 'national poets'.
15. A rapidly increasing number of heavily loaded national symbols and emblems have been typical of the spatiality of this demilitarized Swedish-speaking autonomy on Finnish territory since 1957 when the islands were granted their official flag. In addition, the islands have been given increasing independent participation in certain international bodies. What is more, the autonomous Åland islands can legislate on almost any social and cultural phenomena within its borders. It would be motivated to investigate whether there is by now a surplus of 'Åland' symbols spilling over into the 'Finland-Swedish' category. Also, today the political and legislative autonomy of the Åland islands is known globally and recognized within the international community as a superior example of how to solve minority conflicts in a constructive way.
16. This is, of course, a contrafactual procedure which contributes to the highlighting of what, in Raymond Williams's terms, could be called a particular "structure of feeling". By means of my imaginative move here the quality of the contested spatiality of the Finland-Swedish discourse since its earliest days is emphasized.
17. The museum would be a heterotopia of time, according to Foucault's classification. By providing the illusion that what has been lost to history is still present in the secluded space of the museum, it compensates us for that loss. Heterotopias, claims Foucault, "are linked for the most part to bits and pieces of time" and begin to function "when men find themselves in a sort of total breach of their traditional time" (Foucault 1985–86: 17).
18. The Finnish psychohistorian Juha Siltala (1999) has shown how the Finnish national awakening in the second half of the 19th century built on an image of Finland in which the 'Mother' came to be constituted as that transgressive motivation necessary for the outbreak and persistence of nationalist sentiment. This implied a temporary regression towards the position of the mother within the personality of the individual, however with the collectively productive consequences of bringing a new national culture to life.
19. Sundblom's biographer Johannes Salminen has given major importance to an image which connected Sweden, the sea, motherliness and safety, thus continuing the construction of a cluster of images proposing a lyrical leitmotif of almost transcendental meaning in the life of his subject which, as it seems, was shared by the biographer himself. As a little boy Julius Sundblom used to listen to the waves of the sea rolling slowly against the shores of Hammarudda in the evenings. Asking his father what the sound meant he got the reply that it came from "the calm-sea which brought greetings from the mother country of Sweden". (My transl. Sw. "Det var 'lugn-sjön' som kom med hälsningar från moderlandet Sverige".) This image was lifted onto the clear blue cover of the biography within a square of bright yellow as part of a more extensive extract from the text telling how the child of Julius Sundblom used to climb the mountain of Kasberget by which his home was situated to look out over the landscape in which "the sea (was) flashing as the ultimate border in the West." (My transl. Sw. (...) med havet blänkande till som yttersta gräns i väster). The extract comes from the beginning of chapter one, thus doubly setting the tone for the biography (Salminen 1970: 7). Interestingly, similar aspects of sea imagery appears in Isaksson's biography on Björkman in connection with Nandor Stenlid, who was probably one initiator of the movement for reunion as well as an agent reporting to the Swedish ministry of foreign affairs. Isaksson repeatedly uses the construction "Nandor Stenlid had come over the sea" or similar slightly lyrical expressions to signify a highly prosaic fact throughout a book characterised by an otherwise dry and precise style.

20. Mariehamn: The Provincial Archive of the Åland islands, Carl Björkman's collection, 247/II. Erik Karlsson later took the surname Ramsdahl.
21. There is a similarity with the situation in 1917. Then it would have been the Russian revolution and the Finnish red guards which contributed to Björkman's feeling of threat. In his unpublished autobiographical notes written late in 1938 after his resign, he states that (in 1917) "it was only Swedish sovereignty that would save the small fragment of the Swedish population in the country which was represented by the Åland islands" (My transl. Mariehamn: The Provincial Archive of the Åland islands, Carl Björkman's collection, 261/I). However, in 1938 with the second world war approaching the Åland islands had been autonomous for sixteen years and Björkman found it essential that the islands should manage to protect themselves without Finnish interference. There is accordingly a stronger note of solitude and war rhetoric in his discourse at this date. As his biographer Martin Isaksson has pointed out, Björkman himself indeed helped to create the so-called New Åland Island Question – the question of the armament of the islands – in 1938.
22. (*Uppslagsverket Finland*: 1982: 433). A new edition of the first volume appeared in the year 2003. The remaining volumes are due within the next few years.

References

Bhabha, Homi K. 1994: *The Location of Culture*. London.
Barros, James 1968: *The Aland Island Question: Its Settlement by the League of Nations*. New Haven.
Ekberg, Henrik (ed.) 1982: *Uppslagsverket Finland*. Helsingfors.
Foucault, Michel 1985–86: Other Spaces: The Principles of Heterotopia. In: *Lotus International*: 9–17.
Foucault, Michel 1986: Of Other Spaces. In: *Diacritics*: 22–27.
Isaksson, Martin 1988: *Carl Björkman – Ålands första lantråd*. Helsingfors.
Mazzarella, Merete 1989: *Det trånga rummet: en finlandssssvensk romantradition*. Helsingfors.
Partner, Nancy 1998: Hayden White: The Form of the Content. In: *History and Theory*: 162–172.
Salminen, Johannes 1979: *Ålandskungen*. Helsingfors.
Siltala, Juha 1999: *Valkoisen Äidin Pojat. Siveellisyys ja sen varjot kansallisessa projektissa*. Helsinki.
White, Hayden 1973: *Metahistory. The Historical Imagination in Nineteenth-Century Europe*. Baltimore.
White, Hayden 1982: *The Content of the Form. Narrative Discourse and Historical Representation*. Baltimore.
White, Hayden 1999: *Figural Realism. Studies in the Mimesis Effect*. Baltimore.
Zilliacus, Clas 1991: Om uppodlingen av ett finlandssvenskt symbolträd. In: *Sphinx*: 49–58.
Zilliacus, Clas 2000: I martallsskogen. In: C. Zilliacus (ed.): *Finlands svenska litteraturhistoria*: 37–38.

Religion as a Shelter

Gábor Barna

> Barna, Gábor 2004: Religion as a Shelter. – Ethnologia Europaea 34:1: 71–80.
>
> The custom of donating pictures is still alive in the Franciscan abbey and church at Máriaradna (Arad County, Romania). This provides the possibility of examining the relation between the people and pictures, between the people and the picture collection. In the examined multiethnic, multilingual and multicultural region of the Banat this Roman Catholic tradition of donating pictures has particular symbolic meanings of a religious, ethnic and cultural nature, and is also related to the tolerance shown by the Franciscans towards manifestations of folk religion. The social and mental processes in the past decades in the Romanian Banat could be characterised briefly as: flight from uncertainty and the search for security. Religion and the institutions of religion have a major role in this process.
>
> *Gábor Barna, Ass. Professor, Department of Ethnology and Cultural Anthropology, University Szeged, H-6722 Szeged, Egyetem u. 2. E-mail:barna@hung.u-szeged.hu*

About the Fieldwork

After years of preparation the Department of Ethnology and Cultural Anthropology at the University of Szeged launched a long fieldwork project in the summer of 1996: studying the votive picture gallery at the pilgrimage place of Radna in today's western part of Romania. As a working hypothesis we presupposed that the pictures that play significant roles in the private and community spheres of our everyday life bear symbolic functions. This is especially true for the special places of community life, the sacred places, in our particular case, for the Catholic places of pilgrimage. There are special forms of using pictures here, i.e. the so-called votive pictures and objects. These were donated as votive tokens by believers who wished to underpin their pleas and express their gratitude to the sacred place and the figure worshipped in this sacred place – the Virgin Mary in our case – after their prayers had been heard. The votive object is thus a donation made by the donor as the honouring of a vow, with the request for a special help, or out of gratitude for a grace already bestowed, which the donor takes to the place of pilgrimage or leaves there.[1] The votive object or picture expresses the wish of the person making the vow to be present before the venerated votive image and thus to record himself or herself in eternal prayer. Thirdly, the votive pictures confirm the venerability of the votive image concerned. They recognise the grace and help won there and strengthen the confidence of others in the power of the place. We presupposed that in the examined multiethnic, multilingual and multicultural region of the Banat this Roman Catholic tradition of donating pictures has a particular symbolic meaning of a religious, ethnic and cultural nature.

Folk religion is inconceivable without pictures. Catholicism can be regarded as a religion in which images are especially important.[2] The picture is communication without text and a lasting form of teaching that everyone can understand. The pictures speak in a language that many people understand.[3] Like religious customs and rites in general, the pictures are also a confession of faith.[4] In them the timeless teachings of religion are connected to concrete references linked to time. They show the worldview of a period. However, this worldview is never intimate, but always publicly regulated.[5] The pictures evoke different events of life, they offer the opportunity to recount them again. Portrayal and narrative are thus closely interrelated.[6]

At the site of our research, in Radna the tradition of donating pictures still exists, therefore this practice can be observed, recorded

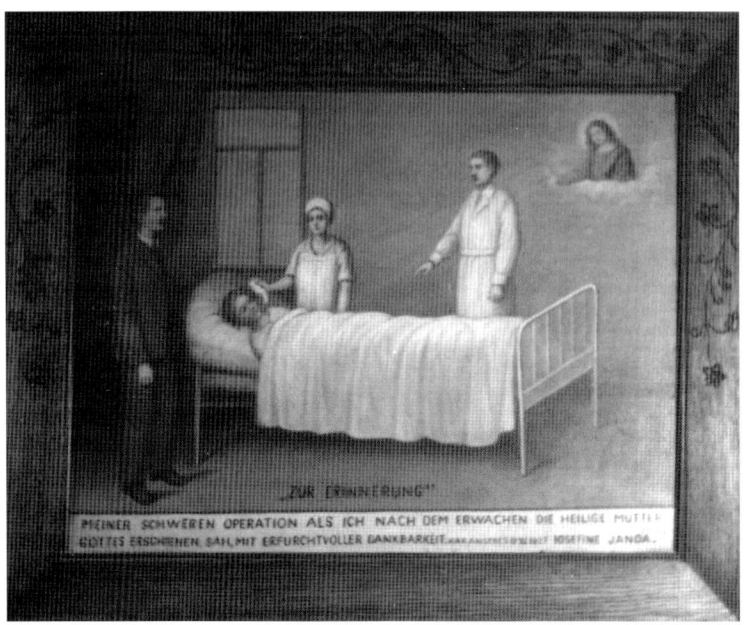

Virgin Mary appears to Josefine Janda. 50,5x63,5, oil, painted inscription in German: "Zur Erinnerung" meiner schweren Operation, als ich nach dem Erwachen die heilige Gottesmutter erscheinen sah. Mit erfurchtvoller Dankbarkeit. Karansebes 17. XI. 1927. Josefine Janda.

and analysed. Further, the people who follow this practice can be interviewed. Thus the relation between the people and pictures and the people and the picture collection can be examined. We believed that the roles of the collection and the place could be observed not only in the everyday religious life but also in the region's society in general.

The Field: The Banat Region – Equilibrium of Differences

In the 16th century the southern part of the Hungarian Kingdom fell under the rule of the Osman-Turkish Empire for nearly two hundred years.[7] It was liberated from the Turkish rule only in 1718 and it is since this time that the area has been referred to as the Banat. The area liberated from the Turks by force of arms was administered for a long while directly from Vienna as an independent administrative unit under the name of Banatus Temesvariensis. The repopulation, recultivation and rejoining of the region in the empire's economic/social life started as a result of the Habsburg military and civil administration.[8] By the 20th century the region had a developed agriculture and industry. These processes and the conscious settlement policy implemented under the auspices of these processes resulted in the multicultural and multilingual image of the Banat in the 18th to 20th centuries.[9] The region had a special position until 1918 in Hungary, then in Romania. Until 1918 the social scene was characterised by the fact that Germans, Hungarians and Romanians lived here in nearly the same number and with the same significance, which meant that despite Romanians being in a relative majority there, no ethnic domination was apparent in the region. This resulted in the emergence of often-cited ethnic tolerance in the region; in the background of which lay economic prosperity besides the ethnic equilibrium. The region's ethnic groups had different functions also in an economic sense and this underpinned and ensured their local role. The settlements – with the exception of the big towns – were generally ethnically homogeneous.

The region was divided between Romania and Serbia by the peace treaty that ended World War One and which dismembered Hungary. With this act a developed Central European region was annexed to the Balkans region, which had a different mentality and was at a different stage of development deriving from its different historical background. A common characteristic feature of the divided (Romanian and Serbian) Banat is that civilisational disagreements and conflicts aggravated.[10] Right after the annexation a large-scale settlement of Orthodox Romanians and Serbs started as well as the expropriation of the local economy, the economic destruction of Germans and Hungarians and their gradual expulsion from the region, which was a way (still supported by the state today) of solving the existing conflicts. The result was a great degree of assimilation among Hungarians and wide dispersion. Following the mass emigration of Germans, after 1990 Romanians from Oltenia and Moldavia moved into the empty villages completely changing the ratio of ethnic groups in the Banat.[11]

Church Administration – Ethnic Groups, Languages, Cultures

The Franciscan Order settled in Lippa (Ger. Lippa, Rom. Lipova) belonging to the Bishopric of Csanád in the 14th century[12]. However, in the 16th century it moved from here to Radna to escape the advancing Turks and has operated here without interruption since then. The monastery and church were rebuilt several times between the 17th and 19th centuries. Up to 1926 the monastery belonged to the Saint John of Capestrano Franciscan province which operated on the Hungarian Great Plain; in that year it was transferred to the Saint Stephen Franciscan province in Transylvania.[13] The Franciscans here were always Hungarians and Germans, as were the believers of the diocese.

Until 1918–1920, the annexation of the region by Romania, despite their minority in number the German and Hungarian ethnic groups were dominant in the Banat. These dominated local and regional administration beside the co-operating local Romanians. After the annexation to Romania, officials from Romania took over the administration and mainly non-Romanians were appointed to the management of various institutions, such as schools and factories. Romanian colonists were settled near the Hungarian settlements that were not considered trustworthy. Romanian border guards were brought into the expropriated houses of Hungarian and German settlements that were in the vicinity of the new Hungarian state border. Also during the so-called land reform Romanians were settled in the lands expropriated from local landowners in order to change the ethnic relations and to intimidate. A mentality very different from the previous one started to spread in the Banat. Corruption and despotism, previously unknown to the Romanian population of the region, poisoned everything.

Ethnic threats were manifested in – beside the excommunication of Hungarians and a smaller number of Hungarophile Germans – the expropriations of homes, romanianising of education, then in an attack against churches and their institutions (orders, church schools). At the end of World War Two our region was also affected by the looting by Romanian independent troops: e.g. the still uninvestigated massacre of a large group of innocent Hungarians at Pîncota (Pankota) and Şiria (Világos, Hellbrunn). The Hungarians of Radna only escaped death by a stroke of luck. Germans were severely affected by their deportation to the Soviet Union, which claimed many thousands of lives and thus decimated their ethnic group. Those who managed to return home faced expropriation and forced organisation of collective farms (kolkhozes). As a result, the relatively closed society of German settlements dissolved. Beside the emigration to Germany after the war, migration to the towns eroded the society of German settlements in the Banat.[14]

The change of ruling power meant a change in the wider community language usage. Formerly, before 1918 the language of administration was Hungarian. Although the ethnic groups were able to use their mother tongue, belonging to Hungary practically meant that Hungarian was the language of the state as well as of individual success in life.[15] However, the Banat was multilingual where the knowledge of Hungarian, German, Romanian and at places Serbian at a high level was quite general. The intermediary languages between different ethnic groups, dominantly Romanian, German and Hungarian as well as smaller groups of Serbs, Croatians, Slovaks, Czechs and Bulgarians were often Hungarian and German.

This situation changed after the annexation of the region to Romania. Romanian became the state language and thus the language of administration and official communication. While in previous decades the Hungarian ethnic group tended to assimilate Germans and in smaller numbers Romanians and other ethnic groups, now the direction of linguistic adjustment and assimilation changed: everybody was assimilated and has been assimilating into the groups of Romanians. This indicates that the individual language/ethnic groups have never been isolated but they were always embedded in a greater society and show that local/micro processes always depended on global/macro processes.

This change in direction did not, however, take place without conflicts since behind the different languages there were and are different cultures and religions, different religious cultures and civilisations.

Child in a craddle with a girl and guardian angel. 41x30, colour print, with a photo of a middle-aged man, handwritten Romanian inscription: Doamne ţie îţi mulţumesc ptr. (=pentru) că maj ajutat ş mai îintinms mina. Gherber Vilhem. Cirka 1910.

The Changes of Identity – Remembering and Remembrance

Few scientific problems have proved to be so long lasting and lengthily intriguing as the issue of identity. It has been the subject of ethnological and sociological researches for many years. Within the next couple of years no drop in interest is expected along the regions of the Danube, either. One reason for this is the tragic history of the nations in the Carpathian Basin in the 20th century: changes in the political systems, collective accountabilities, excommunications, national eradications, ethnic cleansing, multiple border modifications, financial destruction because of loss of wealth, nationalisation and the scattered character of the Hungarian nation. On the other hand, in connection with the accession to the EU the Hungarian nation, which is an odd one out among the other nations in the Carpathian Basin has to deal with the issues of preserving, forming and re-establishing both its own and the European identity.[16]

Remembrance and historical remembering are key elements and founders of individual and community identity creation. Historical remembering is a precise definition of what a community should not forget. Therefore it is not equal to history, it is a selection from history, although its ties to the past are strong. Historical remembrance is not a spontaneous phenomenon and although it is the individual who remembers something and somebody, remembrance is always collective.[17]

Following the partitioning of Hungary as part of the Austro-Hungarian Monarchy after World War One and following the occupation of the dismembered Hungarian lands by the Czechs, Romanians, Serbs and Austrians, the new empire's first task was to destroy the symbols (statues, memorial plaques) of Hungarian remembrance and to exchange them with the objects of another historical remembrance.[18]

The Role of Religion and Churches

We cannot emphasise enough how important Radna is in the sharing of the experienced everyday Catholicism and folk religious practice. Radna with its miraculous picture of the Scapular Blessed Virgin – beside Szeged – is a shrine with a large catchment area in the Great Plain, today divided among three countries. Radna is the sacral centre of a large area's Catholicism.[19] Visiting Radna is a symbolic expression and confession of Catholics belonging together as well as a sign of the unity of the sacral area. According to Sándor Bálint[20], Radna in the 17th and 18th centuries "would be a symbol for Catholicism between Islam and Orthodox religions. (…) Its cultic spell has bound the Hungarian, German, Bunyevci, Bulgarian, Romanian and Tót [= Slovak] people of the Great Plain and Hungary". It cannot have been by chance that after the Romanian occupation the Romanian authorities prevented pilgrimages to Radna. Not only the processions from the truncated Hungary stopped but also the Banat Hungarians and Germans from Serbia stayed away. The motherland dioceses tried to fill or counterbalance this void by getting the Hungarian parts of Radna's catchment area to organise the "Radna procession" in Szeged in the 1920s.[21] The Hungarian pilgrimages by now have been reduced to occasional frequency.

Until World War One Radna was the largest place of pilgrimage of the southern-eastern Hungarian region bordered by Zenta (today Senta, Serbia), Kecskemét, Szolnok, Nagyvárad (today Oradea, Romania), Déva (today Deva, Romania), and Fehértemplom (today Bela Crkva, Serbia), and now it is the biggest shrine in Western Romania. The characteristic feature of the place is the still existing tradition of donating votive pictures that accelerated in the third quarter of the 20th century. The scale of this is illustrated by the 1711 pictures hanging on the corridor walls of Radna's shrine church. The pictures indicate that many of the pilgrims visiting the church felt and still feel that their prayers and pleas are heard here, and with Mary's intercession God has helped them in their troubles and illnesses. They show their gratitude with a picture or a marble plaque. The votive picture gallery is thus continuously growing, changing and expanding.[22]

These donations all prove that the motives behind the purchase and donation of the votive pictures/objects are the same: the individual in a crisis situation can only hope for help from the transcendent world (from God, Mary, saints and angels). He has tried and exhausted all worldly sources of help: physicians, authorities, and other people's empathy. The problems about which these people pleaded for the help of the Virgin Mother of Radna were mainly illnesses,

Virgin Mary and guardian angels helping a child at a car accident. 61x79, oil, handwritten German inscription: Wir danken Dir für unseres Kindes Leben! Du hast es uns jenem Juli Tag 1963 ein zweitesmal gegeben. Den sicheren Tod hätte es unter den Rädern gefunden, hättest du es nicht dem würger Tod mit rettender Hand entwunden, deiner schützenden Hand verdanken wir inneren Flehen, du mögest auch in Zukunft schützend neben uns stehen. Maria hat geholfen. Fam. Freisinger, Glogowatz

The Holy Family in Bethlehem. 24,5x33, colour print, with three photos:
1. couple with child, 2. woman with child, 3. man, with handwritten Romanian inscription: Tatar Maria Măcuţa Sfţintă roagăl pe D-zeu şi pe fiul tău să facă pace întregi mele familii. Cirka 1940.

accidents or problems and conflicts of their individual life that seemed to be impossible to solve. These problems did not, however, originate only from family life conflicts, but they also reflect the social history of the past decades: the war, the lives of the Germans taken to the Soviet Union, the search for stability by the Germans who emigrated to Germany under duress or voluntarily, the helplessness and vulnerability of falsely accused officials in face of the corrupt authorities and the almost last cry for help of the youngster who was not or hardly managed to be accepted at the university. Some interviews contained elements of opposition to the Romanian communist atheist authorities, the fear of them, the expugnability to them and the idea of juxtaposing religion and power. These motives prove that for many people in many situations Radna and the Virgin Mother of Radna, the Catholic religion and faith meant security and the last resort.

The old and young monks of the Radna Franciscan cloister accept and tolerate the religious practice of donating pictures. In the past years though there seem to be changes taking place in the new prelate's acceptance of the practice. Behind the acceptance may lie not only a more tolerant Franciscan way of thinking but also the realisation of the fact that the several hundred pictures in the picture gallery of Radna are all tangible symbols of relying on God, they acknowledge the "last resort" character and role of faith, religion and the church. This was obviously proven by the sharp increase in the number of pictures donated in the times of communism. In the eyes of the visitors the large number of pictures enforce and propagate the effectiveness and popularity of the shrine of Radna.

The tradition of donating pictures therefore lives on in Radna. Its intensity during the past 150 years was changeable. In its outer form the tradition is transformed according to the region's ethnic developments. Over the decades the iconographical composition of the pictures has changed and the language of the messages has also changed. The function of the pictures, however, remained unchanged: they always recall past memories to appear in the present, i.e. the picture makes the past event become present tense. The nature of the pictures and objects as identification and the expression of ethnic identity weakens or disappears. The gallery's pictures will become just signs of intervention by numinosum down here. Although their interpretation becomes increasingly difficult this way, they are still living signs and amplifiers of a peculiar Catholic religious practice. The pictures keep alive a Western Christian religious practice as well as a Central

European, Hungarian, German historical remembrance. These are the roots of the difficulties of the gallery's survival and the clashes with Orthodoxy and the Orthodox Balkan civilisation.

The experiences gained from the Banat fieldwork demonstrate that religion and/or the church and belonging to a church could be the last resort for people in the permanently unstable situation of the twentieth century. It can be a community that provides stability, a hinterland that can mean home and the homeland in a broader sense. This is well illustrated by the fact that the emigrant Germans in their old/new homeland, in today's Germany form and (reconstruct) the sacral space structure that reminds them of their old home, thus they duplicate the sacred place of their old homeland i.e. Radna.[23] The old family house, the cemeteries preserving the ancestors' graves and Radna symbolise the old homeland. The Germans visiting home go to see the old houses they were born in and grew up in, all occupied by strangers (Romanians), they visit the parish church, the cemetery with their ancestors' graves and Radna, the pilgrimage place of the homeland that they left behind. They often brought pictures and photos of their new home in Germany to the Radna picture gallery, thus symbolically unifying the old and new homeland on a sacral level. In the Radna cloister corridor they often look again at the picture they donated, they view the picture gallery and remember, so in this way they help becoming detached spiritually as well.

In the Atmosphere of Instability

One of the lessons to be learnt from the above situation analysis is that in the territory that 84 years ago was divided and annexed between Serbia and Romania new social developments started to take place. These developments are characterised by instability. The new states could not integrate the Banat on the foundations of the previously established system of values and interests. This system was grounded on a civil society of Western Christianity. The countryside previously showing different types of social background for centuries – which was unique even within the Hungarian state framework – could and can only be directed according to the centralising government plans if a permanent feeling of instability is created and sustained. The Western Christian religions and churches in this situation create stability for the individual: they provide a stable base among all the changes and instability. These religions differ from Orthodoxy so their roots are different and when they are connected with ethnic groups they ensure ethnic identity. Therefore they sustain national, religious and language diversity. This way their interests are contrary to the state power's intentions to keep an equilibrium of homogeneity. If the individual is still longing for stability and predictability he will search for and find special ways to achieve these: 1) he will assimilate into the majority ethnic/language/religious/cultural group that provides stability; 2) he will emigrate i.e. he will search for stability in his own majority national/language/group; 3) he will create a transcendent stability in his faith, religion and within the frameworks of his church.[24]

The Holy Family in Nazareth, 28x22, colour print, with photo of a boy, Hungarian inscription: Szűz Anyánk légy velünk. Hálából 1995. Kaplony Máncz család.

Those large-scale changes that characterise the Banat in the 20th century and especially at the end of the century allow for all three possibilities or choices. And those who did not wish to assimilate in either their language or their religion or to emigrate from their native land, found a final refuge in their faith, religion and church. This is expressed symbolically too in the vast collection of votive objects at Máriaradna which, although representing an insignificant proportion of the estimated mass of 1.5–2 million pilgrims over the last century and a half, has a much greater impact because of its nature. It is of special note that the practice of making donations gained new impetus in the 1960s and 1970s, a time when people throughout Romania were most at the mercy of the terror of the Romanian communist dictatorship which penetrated even into their private lives. Almost the only refuge that remained was religion, where faith, humanity, the mother tongue, culture and awareness of self-identity could be preserved. This could not be taken over and controlled by the dictatorship. Individual and community problems could be expressed within the frames of religion. Only religion and the church offered the experience of a true community. But for the individual who placed his trust in God, faith, religion and the church became a point of reference solving his mental problems, easing his civilisational problems and making then tolerable. The creation and survival of the gallery would have been inconceivable without the co-operation of the Franciscans at Máriaradna. It can be said, also on the basis of the interviews conducted with them, that they tolerated the local custom, received and accepted the objects taken to the monastery, especially pictures seeing in them not worthless kitsch and mass-produced articles but the signs of divine grace manifested in the lives of individuals. They interpreted the objects as proof of grace and effective instruments of propaganda.

At the same time these changes are true reflections of the internal dissemination of a once developed and tolerant region. Romania's behaviour after 1920 is that of a typical colonist. The new state took the "native's" wealth away (houses, land, factories), it dispossessed their education and is restricting their churches even today. On the other side it introduced its own language, used exclusively to teach its own history and it supports its own ethnic/state religion. The "natives" are second-rate citizens who can only choose one of the above-mentioned ways to achieve their individual and community stability. If Romania once integrates the Banat, too, they can only do so to the land, since the society that established and for two centuries has sustained and operated the unique culture of the Banat has virtually disappeared: Germans and many Hungarians emigrated and a growing majority of the local society have no local roots, were not born here, they are monolingual and monocultural and they are intolerant. One culture, that of the Germans has already died out.[25] Will the culture of the other nationalities and ethnic groups be next? And as individuals find themselves free of one social constraint (communist dictatorship), now under the influence of another external constraint (globalised capitalist domination), will they be able to form bonds strengthening their security, and to what? Or will all systems of human connections totally disintegrate? Or will the Roman Catholic Church, the Franciscan Order which has always been on the side of the little people and minorities, and the monastery at Máriaradna be able to slow down these processes, if necessary at the price of supporting, tolerating and thereby maintaining the phenomena of folk religion, including in particular the customs of pilgrimage and donating votive pictures – which moreover canon law also regards as something to be preserved[26]? Or will they too, in keeping with the rationalism spreading within the church, discourage pilgrimages and with them the custom of donating votive objects?[27]

Notes

1. Gockerell 1995, 120; Kriss-Rettenbeck 1972, 271–370.
2. Wiebel-Fanderl 1993, 297.
3. Wiebel-Fanderl 1993, 279.
4. In general Oliva Wiebel-Fanderl interprets the role of pictures in everyday life in this way. Wiebel-Fanderl 1993, 278.
5. Wiebel-Fanderl 1993, 278.

6. Wiebel-Fanderl 1993, 278.
7. Engel 1996.
8. Kovách 1998.
9. Bernadett Békési, Bernadett Kiss and Erika Anna Makovics: The Banat in Light of Historical-Statistical Data: The Administrative, Economic and Social History of the Region looks behind these issues citing further literature. For broader historical context see Volgyes 1981, 130–135.
10. Huntington 1998.
11. Bodó 1997; Greffner 1996; Rieser 1992.
12. Lotz 1980.
13. On the history of Máriaradna see: Jordánszky 1836; Balogh 1872; Magyary 1902; Szabó 1921, 324–325; Bálint 1944; Bálint n.d.; Roos 1981; Barna 1991; Roos 1998 with further literature.
14. Cf.: Arnold 2002, and Csóka-Jaksa – Pusztai 2002.
15. Schenk 1978.
16. Goddard – Llobera – Shore 1996, 23–27.
17. Assmann 1999.
18. Barna 2000a; Barna 2000b; Lipták 2000.
19. Bálint – Barna 1994; Roos 1998.
20. Sándor Bálint (1904–1980) professor of ethnography at Szeged university.
21. Bálint 1944, 49–50.
22. ifj. Lele 2000.
23. The quantitative analysis of this collection can be found in the essay in our volume written by Zsuzsánna Péter and Erika Vass.
24. This kind of duplication is not a rare and new phenomenon. Practically the same thing happened in the Middle Ages after Islam conquered the Holy Land: with the use of relics, the holy places of Palestine were re-established in Europe i.e. they were duplicated. A similar process can be observed in the case of the cults forming around icon copies. See: Arnold 2002.
25. Eriksen (1993, 123–124) also considers that from the point of view of ethnic minorities and the state power there are three possibilities: 1) assimilation; 2) accepting the inferior status; 3) separation.
26. Barna – Lönnqvist 2000.
27. Canon 1234, paragraph 2 of the Codex Iuris Canonici provides: "Votive objects displaying folk art and religiosity must be placed visibly in the places of pilgrimage or close to them and must be preserved safely." CIC 1986. 835.

References

András, Károly 1991: Tények, problémák a magyar kisebbségek egyházi életében [Facts and Problems in the Church Life of the Hungarian Minorities living outside Hungary]. *Regio* p2057 Vol. 2. No. 3. 13–37.
Arnold, Erzsébet 2002: A Bánságtól Németországig: a vallási élet változásai a bánsági németek körében [From the Banat to Germany: changes in religious life of the Banat-Germans]. Szeged, szakdolgozat, kézirat. Manuscript.
Assmann, Jan 1999: *A kulturális emlékezet. Írás, emlékezés és politikai identitás a korai magaskultúrákban* [Cultural Remembrance. Writing, Remembering and Political Identity in the Early High Cultures]. Budapest: Atlantisz.
Bálint, Sándor n.d. (1943): *Sacra Hungaria*.
Bálint, Sándor 1944: *Boldogasszony vendégségében* [Visiting the Blessed Mother Mary]. Budapest: Veritas.
Bálint, Sándor & Barna, Gábor 1994: *Búcsújáró magyarok* [Pilgrim Hungarians]. Budapest: Szent István Társulat.
Balogh, Augustus Florianus 1872: *Beatissima Virgo Maria Mater Dei, qua Regina et Patrona Hungariarum*. Agriae.
Barna, Gábor 1991: A kunszentmártoniak radnai búcsújárása [Pilgrimage of the People of Kunszentmárton to Radna]. In: *Magyar Egyháztörténeti Vázlatok* 3, Ed. Horváth, Tibor. Budapest, 209–244.
Barna, Gábor 1997: Religion – Identity – Assimilation. *Acta Ethnographica Hungarica* Vol. 42. Ns. 1–2. 139–148.
Barna, Gábor 1999: Radnai történetek [Stories from Radna]. *Tiszatáj* 8/1999 (August). 45–49.
Barna, Gábor 2000a: Mentale Grenzen – verdoppelte Welten. In: Hirschfelder, Günther; Schell, Dorothea; Schrutka-Rechtenstamm, Adelheid (Hrsg.): *Kulturen – Sprachen – Übergänge. Festschrift für H. Cox zum 65. Geburtstag*. Köln, Böhlau. 643–656.
Barna, Gábor 2000b: A világ megszerkesztése. Szimbolikus és valós vilgok [Designing the World. Symbolic and Real Worlds]. In: Cseri, Miklós, Kósa, László & T. Bereczki, Ibolya (eds.): *Paraszti múlt és jelen az ezredfordulón* [The Past and Present of Peasantry at the Turn of the Century]. Szentendre, Szabadtéri Néprajzi Múzeum – Magyar Néprajzi Társaság, 693–710.
Barna, Gábor & Lönnqvist, Bo 2000: The Lost Future – die expatriierte Kultur. *Schweizerisches Archiv für Volkskunde* 96. 121–143.
Beluszky, Pál 1996: Változó helyünk Európában [Our Changing Place in Europe]. In: Frisnyák, Sándor (ed.) *A Kárpát-medence történeti földrajza* [The Historical Geography of the Carpathian Basin]. Nyíregyháza: Bessenyei György Tanárképő Főiskola, 77–96.
Bodó, Barna 1997: Azonosulás, elitek, peremlét [Assimilation, the Elite, Marginal Existence]. *Kisebbségkutatás* Vol. 6. No. 4. 418–444.
Downs, Roger M. & Stea, David 1982: *Kognitive Karten. Die Welt in unseren Köpfen*. New York: Harper and Row Publishers.
Engel, Pál 1996: *A temesvári és moldovai szandzsák törökkori települései* (1554–1579) [The Turkish Era's Settlements in the Sanjaks of Temesvár and Moldova 1554–1579]. Szeged: Csongrád Megyei Levéltár.
Eriksen, Thomas Hylland 1993: Ethnicity and Nationalism. Anthropological Perspectives. London:

Pluto Press.

Gilberg, Trond 1981: Modernization, Human Rights, Nationalism: The Case of Romania. In: George Klein & Milan J. Reban (eds.): *The Politics of Ethnicity in Eastern Europe*. East European Monographs. New York: Boulder 185–211.

Gockerell, Nina 1995: *Bilder und Zeichen der Frömmigkeit. Sammlung Rudolf Kriss*. München.

Goddard, Victoria A., Llobera, Josep R. & Shore, Cris 1996: Introduction: The Anthropology of Europe. In: Goddard, Victoria A., Llobera, Josep R. & Shore, Cris: *The Anthropology of Europe. Identities and Boundaries in Conflict*. Oxford: Berg. 1–40.

Greffner, Otto 1996: *Das Banat und die Banater Schwaben. Kurzgefasste Geschichte einer deutschen Volksgruppe*. Weil am Rhein.

Huntington, Samuel P. 1998: *A civilizációk összecsapása és a világrend kialakulása* [The Clash of Civilisations and the Emergence of a World Order]. Budapest: Európa Kiadó.

Jordánszky Elek 136 *Magyar országban, 's az ahoz tartozó részekben lévő Bóldogságos Szűz Mária kegyelem' képeinek rövid leírása* [Short Description of the Miraculous Pictures of the Virgin Mary which Can Be Found in the Hungarian Kingdom and Countries Belonging to It]. Pest.

Kovách, Géza 1998: *A Bánság demográfiai és gazdasági fejlMése (1716sh 1848)* [The Demographic and Economic Development of the Banat 1716–1848]. Szeged: Csongrád Megyei Levéltár

Kriss-Rettenbeck, Lenz 1972: *Ex Voto, Zeichen, Bild und Abbild im christlichen Votivbrauchtum*. Zürich: Atlantis.

ifj. Lele, József 2000: Radnai búcsú – Szegeden [The Radna Pilgrimage Festival – in Szeged]. In: L. Imre, Mária (ed.): *Népi vallásosság a Kárpát-medencében* [Vernacular Religiousness in the Carpathian Basin]. Pécs: Baranya Megyei Múzeumok Igazgatósága. 200–206.

Lendvai L. Ferenc 1997: *Közép-Európa koncepciók* [Central European Concepts]. Budapest, Áron Kiadó.

Lipták, L'ubomir 2000: *Helycserék a piedesztálokon*. [Changing Places on the Pedestals]. Kalligram: Pozsony, 244–292.

Lotz, Antal 1984: Szeged-csanádi egyházmegye [The Diocese of Szeged-Csanád]. In: Turányi, László (ed.) *Katolikus almanach* [Catholic Almanac] 1984. Budapest. 751–757.

Magyary, Pál 1902: *Mária-Radna és a Boldogságos Szt. Szűz kegyelmes képének története némi kegyelmek és csodák felsorolásával* [Mária-Radna and the History of the Miraculous Pisture of the Gracefull Virgin Mary with Mentioning of Some Graces and Miracles]. Temesvár.

Pándi, Lajos 1995: *Köztes-Európa 1763–1993* [Europe in Between 1763–1993]. Budapest: Osiris.

Rieser, Hans-Heinrich 1992. *Temeswar. Geographische Beschreibung der Banater Hauptstadt*. Sigmaringen.

Roos, Martin 1981: Maria-Radna. In: *Das Banat und die Banater Schwaben*. Bd. 1. München, 33–39.

Roos, Martin 1998: *Maria-Radna. Ein Wallfahrtsort in Südosten Europas 1*. Regensburg: Schnell und Steiner.

Schenk, Annemie 1978: Schule und Bildung bei Sozialisierungsprozessen am Beispiel ethnischer Gruppen des Banats. In: Weber-Kellermann, Ingeborg (Hrsg.) *Zur Interethnik. Donauschwaben, Siebenbürger Sachsen und ihre Nachbarn*. Frankfurt a.M. 326–340.

Szabó, György Piusz 1921: *Ferencrendiek a magyar történelemben. Adalékok a magyar ferencrendiek történetéhez* [Franciscans in the Hungarian History. Date to the History of Franciscans in Hungary]. Budapest.

Tánczos, Vilmos 1997: Hányan vannak a moldvai csángók? [How Many Csángos Are There in Moldavia?]. *Magyar Kisebbség, Nemzetpolitikai Szemle*. New series 3rd year, issue 1–2. (7–8.). 370–390.

Volgyes, Ivan 1981: Legitimacy and Modernization. Nationality and Nationalism in Hungary and Transylvania. In: Klein, George – Reban, Milan J. (eds.) *The Politics of Ethnicity in Eastern Europe*. East European Monographs, New York: Boulder. 127–146.

Wiebel-Fanderl, Oliva 1993: *Religion als Heimat?* Wien: Böhlau Verlag.

Zalatnay István 1991: Etnikai közösség: kihívás és feladat az egyházak számára régiónkban [Ethnic Community: A Challenge and a Task for the Churches in Our Region]. *Regio* Vol. 2. No. 3. 3–12.

The Symbolic Order of Gender in Academic Workplace

Ways of Reproducing Gender in Equality within the Discourse of Equality[1]

Paula Mählck

> Mählck, Paula 2004: The Symbolic Order of Gender in Academic Workplace. Ways of Reproducing Gender in Equality within the Discourse of Equality. – Ethnologia Europaea 34:1: 81–96.
>
> It is well known that universities are male dominated both in history as well as in the dominant discourses. As knowledge producing organizations universities also carries the heritage of defending the scientific ethos of meritocracy and objectivity, these are rules that many researchers still are trained to believe in. This makes often studying of gender inequality in academia a difficult task since it not only reveals the gendered structures of academia but also violates the norms of science implying that science is socially biased. This article explores how gender inequality is produced within the discourse of equality at Swedish universities. The underlying assumption is that gender inequality on the level of the academic departments is produced within the broader discourses of gender, power, science and equality operating in everyday academic working lives and in society in general.
>
> *Paula Mählck, PhD. Mälardalens University / ISB, Box 883, S–721 23 Västerås.*
> *E–mail: paula.mahlck@mdh.se*

Introduction and Earlier Works

In 1995 the UN declared Sweden the best country in the world for women to live in according to a Gender and Development Index (GDI) (UNDP:1995). As a small Nordic welfare state Sweden offers a quite privileged setting when it comes to gender distribution in higher education. The total gender distribution within higher education was forty-eight percent women and fifty two percent men in 2000. However the gender distribution differs between different staff categories. Women represent a majority of the staff involved in administration and teaching. For positions that are more extensively designed for research such as research assistants and full professors, women are still in the minority. Thirty eight percent of the research assistant positions and thirteen percent of the full professorships are held by women (National Agency for Higher Education yearbook 2001). Thus, we can see that within the domain of higher education Sweden follows the international pattern of "The leaking pipeline", the higher up in the academic hierarchy the fewer the women and the more the men. This has led to a wide range of efforts aimed at diminishing gender differences in academic career achievement. In some cases it has resulted in different equality positions such as, equal opportunities officers and equal opportunity committees. Nowadays, formal ways of excluding or diminishing women in academia are no longer accepted and it is highly unlikely that someone would openly declare that women are inferior to men when it comes to pursuing a research career. However, research has shown that gender differences in scientific careers still remain despite the introduction of equal opportunity policies. Gender marked inequalities are documented in the distribution of scholarships as well as in gender difference in career achievement (Winnifred and Hamilton 1988, Stolte Heiskanen 1991, Wold and Wennerås

1997). In order to increase our insight as to why gender differences in academic careers[2] persist, research about how the gender order[3] is produced and reproduced in everyday academic working life, needs to be elaborated.

This article explores the production and reproduction of the symbolic order of gender at different levels in the academic workplace. The underlying assumption is that gender relations exist within the broader discourses of gender, power, science and equality operating in the academic department and at a general level of society. The aim of this article is to explore "How gender inequality on the level of the academic department is reproduced within the discourse of equality operating at a general level of society". The field of study is two academic departments in the same area of biology at two different Swedish universities.

Previous research about gender differences in scientific careers has produced numerous explanations. Very briefly these can be categorized into three main groups; "gender differences in publication productivity", "impact of family situation on scientific careers" and "the social organization of science, The Old Boys Network" (Fox and Faver 1985, Luukonen-Gronow 1987, Davis and Astin 1990, Cole and Zuckerman 1991, Kyvik 1991, Long 1993, Sonnert and Holton 1995). The results have often been contradictory and cover a wide range of methodological and theoretical approaches. However, previous research has not gone without criticism and three main lines have emerged over the years. Firstly, the need for studying gender differences in scientific careers over a longer time perspective has been expressed, since women appear to have different career trajectories with more "winding tracks" than men (Elgquist-Saltzman 1994). Secondly, there is a risk that focusing on gender differences when studying scientific careers leads to an essentialist trap where differences are emphasized and reproduced. Thus, it is important to focus on the construction of femininity and masculinity and by which means differences are constructed, legitimized and reproduced. Thirdly, since a scientific career most probably depends on a cumulative effect of a multitude of factors interacting over time, further studies of the complex interactions between and within individuals in their daily research milieu are called for. In the following discussion the theoretical framework of this study is further outlined.

Theorizing Gender

Gender is often described as the social dimension of biological sex; this is particularly evident in the famous statement "you are not born a woman, rather you become one" (de Beauvoir 1949). Since these words were first written the social construction school has developed different theoretical lines and gained acceptance both within and outside of feminist readings[4]. The following offers one definition of gender:

"*Gender*, refers to patterned, socially produced, distinctions between female and male, feminine and masculine. Gender is not something people are, in some inherent sense, although we may consciously think of ourselves in this way. Rather, for the individual and the collective it is a daily accomplishment (West & Zimmerman 1987) that occurs in the course of participation in work organizations as well as in many other locations and relations" (Acker 1992: 250).

In this article the social construction perspective also includes the body and physical appearance as well as sexuality, which are all part of the ongoing production of gender. The notion of power is central when conceptualizing gender since patterned differences between women and men, femininity and masculinity usually involve various expressions of the subordination of women (Acker 1992). Thus, it is important to remember that these power relations are further complicated when factors such as race and class are intertwined with gender. The gender order can be challenged if the rigidity of the male/female dualism is challenged and the notion of difference is nuanced and contextualised (Gherardi 1995: 101–103).

Within the social construction school some have focused on the relational aspect of gender; this interpretation emphasizes the mutual inter-relational construction of femininity and masculinity as well as the importance of contextual and processual aspects on the construction of gender (Gherardi 1995, Davies 1996). The relational aspect of gender focuses on the "doing of gender" and consequently on the meanings that spring from the "doing of gender", as well as the conditions and contexts surrounding this process. This raises the question of how gender is *represented* in our daily lives or, more precisely, how we give meaning to gender through language, action and symbols. This has been elaborated in theories of representation which, very briefly, can be said to deal with the processes by which subjects of a specific culture and historical context use language, or any signifying system, to produce meaning (Hall 1997: 61).

Representing Gender

Theories of representation include a wide range of approaches, from semiotics to discourse[5]. In this article the broader concept of *discourse* is used rather then a more narrow use of language that a linguistic approach would require. In this article discourse not only includes what one says (language) but also what one does (practice). In this sense discourses not only "defines" how we can talk about certain topics but also influences how ideas are put into practice and used to regulate the conduct of others (Hall 1997: 44). Foucault was one of the first to introduce the notion of discourse instead of language in the production of meaning. Stuart Hall defines discourse as

"[…] a group of statements which provide a language for talking about – a way of representing knowledge about – a particular topic at a particular historical moment" (Hall 1992: 291 in Hall 1997: 44).

According to Foucault our perception of what constitutes the "truth" in certain historical moments and contexts contribute to the maintenance and internalization of dominant discourses in our everyday lives. This is what Foucault calls regime of truth. The regime of truth is constituted by a discursive formation[6] that legitimizes what is perceived as true or false, the means for doing so and the status of persons who are in charge of this activity. Foucault's puts it like this:

"Each Society has its regime of truth, its 'general politics' of truth, that is, the types of discourses which it accepts and makes function as true, the mechanisms and instances which enable one to distinguish true and false statements, the means by which each is sanctioned… the status of those who are in charge with saying what counts as true" (Foucault 1980: 131).

Applied to gender studies this theoretical approach implies that a regime of truth, that is sustained by discursive formations and consequently are relative to historical, situational and contextual aspects, makes it possible to internalized dominant discourses about gender. This influences how agents act and give meaning to gender in their everyday lives, in other words, how they discursively produce and reproduce gender in their everyday lives.

The Dual Presence

In general the history of science has been male dominated in numbers as well as in the dominant discourses (Keller 1985). This is also reflected in the symbolic order of gender. One set of qualities such as reason and public presentation, qualities associated with science as well as with activities in the public sphere in general have been associated with masculinity. Qualities associated with emotions and private activities have been associated with femininity, reproduction and the private sphere. In this perspective women will always be "lacking" important qualities when entering the professional scene. Thus, women entering the professional arena are still symbolically connected to qualities associated with the domestic sphere, and the gender order from the private sphere has been transferred to the public sphere (Marshall and Wetherell 1989, Wager 1994, Katila and Meriläinen 1999). This phenomenon is often described as the "dual presence" of women which indicates a cross gender experience, more specifically the simultaneously presence of the private and the public, home and work, personal and political (Balbo 1979; in

Gherardi 1994: 598). Managing dual presence requires different discursive strategies.

Gherardi has identified two different types of strategies that are used for handling "dual presence"; she calls them ceremonial and remedial work. In ceremonial work, differences between sexes are recognized and celebrated which can be done in a number of ways, for example through gestures, tones or language. It is very difficult to avoid ceremonial work since gender is one of the major social categorizations that we use in our everyday life. It is also deeply imbedded in what we call "good manners"; to avoid celebrating gender is often seen as odd and sometimes rude behavior. Celebrating gender can also involve a sense of pleasure. When interacting with other people celebrating and responding to gender can create a sense of belonging to the "bigger" bodies, or with Foucault's words, to the "discursive formations" of the feminine and the masculine.

When the dual presence occurs there is a break in the gender order and this requires other rituals. This is where the remedial work enters the scene. Remedial work is "simultaneously supportive of the symbolic order of gender and remedial of the offence" (Gherardi 1994: 602). When women enter public organizational life they break the symbolic order of gender. Through remedial work women can enter public life and still celebrate conventional femininity. This can be done by working in female dominated areas or by adjusting gestures and language. Gherardi gives the following example of remedial work:

"When women take the conversational initiative and apologize for doing so, when she expresses her doubts as to the importance of what she is about to say, when she minimizes her competence to speak on the subject – that is, when she requests authorization, protection and benevolence" (1994: 605).

Data and Method

The empirical data comes from two departments at two different universities specializing in the same area of biology. Biology was chosen because several studies indicates that women at biology departments have passed a threshold that attenuate gender stratification (Long 1993, Sonnert and Holton 1995). Twelve interviews of two types were conducted. The questions were loosely structured, with interviews lasting between 90 and 120 minutes. When needed, a second interview was arranged. All interviews were recorded, with the consent of the interviewed person, and all have been transcribed. The interview quotes in this article have been translated into English by the author.

The first type of interviews was conducted with senior researchers who were asked questions about the research organization, policymaking, dissemination of information etc. My intention was to get an overview of the organization of the department as well as a glimpse at its specific culture. The second type of interview was conducted with "new researchers" that rather recently had finished their PhD. The original ambition was to interview researchers that were within the first years of receiving their PhD degree. However, finding researchers matching these criteria was not easy and in some cases the time period had to be expanded. The "new researchers" were asked questions about personal background, ambitions and future plans, faculty advisor relationships, access to information, collaboration and support and other questions concerning how they perceived their everyday working life.

When working with a qualitative method and the material that comes along with it a researcher is often asked questions about he or she can be certain they are getting the "true story". Naturally, it is extremely difficult to answer such a question; it would require a more psychological approach and even then it would remain highly problematic. Rather than dwelling on the issue I have preferred to see it from a different perspective; people create different stories when they answer the questions and this is a way of affirming their identity/ies. I have acknowledged the diversity, ambiguity and fragmented dimensions of the stories because they represent their lived experiences and are true for them. My interest lies in the *form* of these stories, more precisely, how the interviewed researchers present the stories, rather than trying to explore which story is the "true" one[7]. It is also important to recognize the power dimension of my position as a researcher and that the interview situation is a rather extreme situation for both the researcher interviewing and the one being interviewed. However, the underlying assumption is that knowledge is situated[8] and that identities are multiple and continuing constructs, which implies that there is no "inner core" that represents a true version of what a person really think or believes.

Results and Analysis

Situating the Researchers[9]

At a first glance it is very easy to find similarities between the two departments; they belong to the same academic discipline so it is natural to expect that they share some structural constraints and possibilities. The research field is characterized by a quite good financial situation, at least compared to the humanities and the social sciences. Also, it does not belong to the pure applied technological and medical research areas where the funding situation must be considered to be better. Findings in the field have short life span and research development and research innovations become old news very fast. This most likely goes hand in hand with the use of/dependence on advanced technological equipment, something that is increasing. It is also reasonable to believe that the departments share the same research organization since most natural sciences are organized in research teams due to practical and economic reasons. Peters and Vanraan's (1991) study found that the internal co-authorship networks of a chemical engineering department centered on a few productive scientists and formed clusters. At our departments the researchers and PhD students were organized in teams based on research orientation. A "typical" research team consisted of a PhD research leader, sometimes a post-doc, and (at least) one or two doctoral students. In some cases the group also had their own laboratory assistant, which depended on their financial situation. However, a closer look at the departments revealed that they were differently structured by gender, academic position and research areas.

In Department A I found that four research groups were active. The department had one elderly male professor who was the research leader of one group, which did not appear to influence the power balance between the research groups. Since academia is a hierarchical institution it is natural to expect certain hierarchies such as those between PhD students and PhDs, however hierarchy between the research group leaders and the professor was not stressed in the interviews. The research groups appeared to be equally influential; no research orientation (or group) appeared to be more central or peripheral, or have more or less status than another. Below Howard, a senior researcher describes the seminar distribution and guest research distribution between the different research groups/ areas.

"We try to divide it up so that everyone has the same number. We are all very different but we try to divide it so that there is something for everyone. I mean, it would never happen that there would be a seminar series in my area only, that would be pointless.[...] Even if we're all different I'd have to say that we complement each other in a way."

Bill, a new researcher describes the department the following way:

"[...] There's a good atmosphere between the senior researchers, they don't compete for the doctoral students, there's an alternating system. [...] So there's no friction between them like there might be at other places. They've built up a pretty simple system for who gets what and then if there are any objections, it seems to work anyway. So the atmosphere is relatively, it's a pretty good group of people."

Collaboration between the research groups did occur although the groups had their own distinct research areas and consequently the collaboration mostly concerned methodological issues. Sex distribution appeared to be equal at both doctoral student level as well as research leader level; two of the four research groups were headed by women.

In Department B research was similarly

organized in research groups. However, the department was much more male dominated both at doctoral student level and at research leader level. The department had two male professors with strong positions, both as social and cognitive leaders. The formal structures for decision-making were well established but there also seemed to be informal structures in those processes. Edward, a new researcher describes the department the following way:

"[…] But it's pretty established, I think in comparison with other departments, formal democracy, departmental meetings once a month where important matters are discussed and prepared for the department board meetings where the decisions are made. Then it's like this, many important decisions are made in smaller informal groups. […] But of course, our current second professor and department head is there, and before it was the older professor who took the initiative. He'd been here for so long, so he had a lot of power at the department until he went part time, then it became a bit more decentralized when the other professor took over being the head of department. He didn't have the same ambition to make all the decisions like the older professor did. Because, if you're both professor and department head for a long time then of course you make most of the decisions on your own. Even if it was he who started with the departmental meetings, in some way it really only gives the impression of democracy."

In this quotation we can see that although the department has become a bit more decentralized since the second professor has become the head of the department he still has a strong position. Edward also highlights that decision-making often takes place in informal groups outside the formal structures of the department. Status differences between research groups and research orientations were clearly expressed when describing the research activity at the department. The closer to the professor in terms of social and cognitive positions the higher status the researchers had. The department had six research groups but their research orientations were slightly more homogenous than at Department A. Only one research group appeared to have less collaboration with the others. That group also appeared to have less status than the others. The female research leader of that group also reported that she lacked collaboration partners at the department, felt excluded from the inner circles of the departments and had difficulties getting access to informal information although she was a senior researcher and member of the department board.

Researchers at both departments were very keen on stressing their enthusiasm towards gender equality in academia. They were aware of the higher level of dropouts of female academics and offered several explanations for this They had also developed equality plans for achieving equal sex distribution at all levels of the departments.

Formal ways of excluding or diminishing women in higher education are no longer accepted and the introduction of equality positions has among other things assured the discourses of equality between women and men in academia. Presently, it is unlikely that somebody would openly declare women as less suited than men for pursuing an academic career. This does not mean that gender inequality does not exist in academia. The diminishing of female academics is expressed in more subtle ways that are imbedded in everyday working situations. This has led to a debate about the possibilities and practices of the rhetoric of equality. This will not be further developed here. The main point is instead; how is inequality reproduced within a discourse of equality? Researchers were asked by me to describe what they thought the reasons for gender differences in career achievement in academia were and more particularly within the field of biology.

Turning Positive Stereotypes into Grounds for Exclusion

A male researcher, lets call him Andy, who is still active within academia doing research in Department A, which appeared to be less male dominated, less centralized and less hierarchical than department B. Andy is married and has no children. His wife is not a researcher. In the following quotation Andy answers to the following question: "Do you think it is easier for men than for women to pursue an academic career after receiving the PhD degree?"

"Within this area of biology we have fairly equal numbers of women and men taking undergraduate courses as well as at the doctoral student level. At the moment and at this department that's also the case at research assistant level. It's is not statistically proven but I guess that the situation is fairly equal. They [women: my remark] have not been able to make it all the way to the top but it takes time. I don't think [there is a difference: my remark]. One difference is that women are away on parental leave longer, so the reasons should be looked for at home rather than at work. No, I can't see that women have been discriminated against in academia, at least not here, I couldn't speak for other countries, but I haven't seen anything, at least not here. The difference is above all at home. Maybe women are not so manic as men are. [...] They're not prepared to sacrifice as much. I mean, very few have "normal" working days and it's very hard to advance if you have small children. That's just the way it is. I wouldn't be able to work as much if I had children. [...] You could put it like this, you have to have the brains but there's nothing that can replace hard work. That's the way it is, so there's a tendency towards people who work a lot."

Time plays a significant role in explaining gender differences in academic careers in this quote and is referred to at two levels. Firstly, time is found on a structural level: "They [[women]] have not been able to make it all the way to the top but it takes time." This reasoning suggests that gender differences in scientific careers persist due to old values and perspectives, old ways of doing gender. Thus, it assumes that present ways of doing gender are unproblematic and leaves them intact. The stressing of time as an explanatory factor for gender inequality appears in other studies concerning gender equality in political representation as well (Tollin 1998:30). Secondly, it is present on a micro level, as a part of the labor division within families: "One difference is that women are away on parental leave longer, so the reasons should be looked for at home rather than at work". This puts the focus on processes outside of academia; however, it also tends to individualize gender differences in scientific careers. The focus is on situations within families rather than on structural constrains in the system of higher education. Although the concept of "parental leave" is used, it soon becomes obvious that what is implied is in fact motherhood, "women are a way on parental leave longer". To refer to motherhood is to refer to women's reproductive capabilities and thus to stress the biological differences between female and male researchers. To stress gender differences as binary oppositions is a common way of producing and reproducing the gender order (Hirdman 1988). The ties between parents and children carry strong connotations regarding what is perceived as "natural"; however there are also has "positive" connotations. This legitimizes the differences in career achievement between researchers that have children and researchers without children but has an even stronger legitimizing effect on gender differences in scientific careers since motherhood is a major way of constructing femininity. Gender differences in career achievement is thus, deferred to "natural" and "positive" processes of motherhood and leaves the structures of the academic career system intact and seen as unproblematic.

Later in the interview a second explanation is introduced: "maybe women are not as manic as men are". To be manic is to be in a negative mental condition or have a mental disease. At first glance this may appear flattering for female researchers: they are not as "manic" (sick) as men are. However, this quote also reveals that succeeding in academia is hard, in fact so hard that in order to succeed you must be able to break the "natural" and "positive" ties of parenthood. "Manic" is constructed negatively, breaking the ties of parenthood, but at the same time positively, being able to work hard and being ambitious, attributes that are normally used to describe good researchers. "Manic" appears to have been transformed and is now used as a positive indicator for being successful in academia. In the quote above we could see that "manic" was associated with men. However, "manic" also includes the separation between the private and the professional: "I wouldn't be able to work as much if I had children". Management studies have shown that separating the private from the public and, thus, constructing women as a negation of the norm is a major obstacle for women's efforts to reach top positions within organizations (Kanter 1977, Cockburn 1991, Wahl *et al*. 1998). This reasoning rests on the dualistic relationship between femininity and masculinity, the private and the public, the irrational and the rational. In addition it can be said that while being a successful researcher reinforces male gender identity it implies a contraction for female researchers' gender identity.

The concept of "manic" appears to be central for the understanding of how Andy makes sense of gender differences in scientific careers. Let us therefore take a look at how he uses the concept in other situations. In the following quote Andy was asked if he had any intellectual role models in science.

"My biggest intellectual role model was probably my external supervisor. His extreme tattering and torning of all theories, it was almost self-destructive. [...] The ones that have succeeded in science normally have bad personal lives so you really don't want to be compared with them. So if I compare myself with those who have really succeeded in science, those who have build up megalomaniac organizations, I wouldn't like to change places with them, because they really are totally manic about what they do."

In the first quote we could see how "manic" was transformed to mean something positive, particularly in relation to women who were not as "manic" as men. In this latter quote the researcher is comparing himself to the scientific elite, and in relation to them "manic" is constructed negatively: "I wouldn't like to change places with them, because they really are totally manic about what they do". In addition, we can se how Andy uses the concept of manic to construct himself positively in relation to both groups; he paints a picture of himself as professionally and intellectually superior to women and emotionally superior compared to the scientific elite. However, a second glance at this reasoning suggests criticism against the academic career system. "Manic" is constructed negatively as is the scientific elite, which implies that the researcher perceives the academic system as hostile towards those who can not put up with the harsh working conditions, particularly women and women and men with children.

From the quotations we can see that Andy is ambivalent towards gender in academic workplaces. In a daily working environment where females are present as high productive research leaders having both families, children and an academic career, the symbolic order of gender is not easily legitimized and thus, requires other rituals for making sense of everyday working life. The construction of a researcher as someone that is totally devoted to academia and has no family obligations can bee understood as one way of reproducing the gender order and making sense of gender in academic workplaces.

The interviewed researchers in this study most certainly perceive themselves, as "pro-gender equality" and thus, their aim is to speak within the discourse of gender equality. As pointed out earlier it is unlikely that someone would openly declare women as less suited than men for pursuing an academic career. However, the changed discourse of "manic" from negative to a positive indicator for a successful researcher, and the construction of women as "lacking" has done this in a more subtle way.

The quotes above were chosen because they eloquently provided answer to my research questions, however other women and men from both departments expressed similar opinions. The quotations below give further insights into how the researchers understand gender differences in scientific careers. The following quote comes form Andy's supervisor Howard who is a senior researcher at Department A. Below he gives his explanation as to why there are fewer women pursuing an academic career.

"Of course it may in part be because women are less forward than men, even if they have the same qualifications but I also think that it boils down to society. What they hell are you going to do when that's standard, when women are expected to stay home ten months with the baby and the man stay home two months? I mean right there there's a difference. I mean, society has to solve the problem. Instead of the women doing as well at research as men and at the same time doing more at home. It doesn't make sense."

Later he describes the success of the female senior researchers at his department in the following way.

"It's all by chance. You can't have a small department and start drawing grand conclusions. It's just turned out so, it just so happens that both Miranda and Isabel are doctoral students from here. They've succeeded, I guess you could say it's luck that we've had two bright doctoral students that have shown, in Miranda's case she had no children so in her case I guess you could say that she's been able to act like a man in that way. Isabel has succeeded with three kids and I really respect that. But I think she has a husband who does a lot at home. So I really think, I blame society, no not society but the attitude in society. I don't think that it'll get any better before women have true equality, at home. How the hecks else are they supposed to succeed at the job if they don't, if they do everything, more than 80–90 percent at home."

Howard suggests two explanations for women's poorer academic career output. First he suggests that women are less pushy than men and second he situates the problem to the private sphere. He uses the term society but it becomes clear that he is talking about the researchers' family situation. It is also interesting to note that he refers to the notion of coincidence when referring to the success of his female colleagues. It is unclear whether he means that their success is due to coincidence or if it is a coincidence that they were trained at his department.

The following quote is from Amanda who is married to a researcher and has several children. Amanda has also been a doctoral student under Howard but she left the department after completing her PhD.

"Yes, but the problem is that they're cutting back and just when I was finished and was about to defend my thesis, or just when I went on maternity leave, and I didn't want to stay. I saw these women who struggled with their seventy-five percent work time and who had children and didn't have time for it all and who were researchers too. And it was them who ended up staying at home when the children were sick and I mean, you fall behind on the research front and it really is pretty tough being a woman, and being a woman and a researcher. So I just felt like the pressure was too much both at home and at work. Very few know that they have research money and whether they have a position. There are so few permanent positions at the university."

Amanda has mainly been teaching during the past seven years. She is currently working as a teacher at a college and has ambitions to combine research and teaching. Amanda states that she did not want to stay at the department after she had her baby. We can see that Amanda is referring to women's double workload combining family life with an academic career. Amanda is also critical of the structures of academia that offer so few tenured positions. As we can see Amanda points at several processes influencing gender differences in academic careers as compared to Andy and Howard who mainly stressed the family situation of researchers. Researchers that had small children seemed to be more inclined to alternate between different explanations that sometimes included processes in the family situation of researchers, or processes included in the everyday life of academia, when explaining gender differences in academic careers. Later in the interview Amanda also reported that she had felt like an outsider while pursuing her PhD. She had felt invisible and experienced that her supervisor ignored her in favor of a male PhD student which made her feel discouraged.

Irene did her research training in Department B and is now working as a senior researcher at another department. Irene gives the following explanation for why there are gender differences in academic careers. Irene is married to a researcher and has several children.

"Well, often the women will say that they're not

prepared to invest so much, or don't think they have time, or that it's not so much fun that they have the energy for it all. I mean, it's very unusual that someone at that level will say they're stupid. If you've gotten your PhD you don't say you're stupid because you're not, or else you would never have gotten your PhD. No, it's more that, you don't say that you aren't good enough because you're stupid, but because you don't want to spend so much time, or because it ends up hurting the kids. Or because there are other things in life too. I felt that way, when I was at the end of my rope, I thought, God it would be nice if I didn't get any research funding, then I wouldn't have to deal with this rubbish, and maybe it's wrong to call it self-censorship, it's maybe not being prepared to pay the price. Not that the men have said that we shouldn't (laugh) but because you actually don't want to. Because it's just not worth the high price. I guess that's being a negative role model, a female professor at the department who's a negative role model, hard on oneself and on those around her."

Irene states that it is not due to intellectual inabilities that women leave academia. Instead she points at the harsh working conditions in academia and women being less willing to "pay the price". Irene also suggests that this is a common explanation among women. This makes sense since the construction of women as lacking can shift into an overvaluation of femininity, particularly when constructing motherhood. This can also be interpreted as criticism against the academic system. She refers to a female professor who is "*hard*" on herself and on the people in her surroundings, a negative role model.

In the quotes above we can see how women are constructed as lacking in a positive sense, "not being willing to pay the prize" or "valuing the family higher than a career". Thus, the lacking in a negative sense, that is to devaluate women, tend to shift into overvaluation of the same, but both discourses are exclusionary. We can also see that researchers with children are more inclined to mention different factors as obstacles varying from family situation to the structures of academia when they talk about gender in academic workplaces.

One tentative explanation for why the discourse of the impossibility of combining motherhood with an academic career seems to be prominent when explaining gender differences in academic careers is that in such a discourse the problem is both individualised and placed outside academia. Focusing on internal processes in academia would imply criticism of the structure of academia and would therefore require collective action for change.

Internalization of Inferiority – Superiority through Paternalism

This section offers different examples of how paternalism coexists with the discourse of gender equality when making sense of gender differences in academic careers. The first quote comes from Irene quoted above and the second is from Stanley who is also from Department B. Let us begin with Irene. Irene was asked: "Do you think it is easier for men than for women to pursue an academic career after PhD exam?" She answers the question by telling a story about a female colleague of hers.

"Where I work now, there is a female researcher. When she received tenure after her PhD, she hadn't planned to continue after PhD. [...]but by chance a tenured position became available and her previous supervisor encouraged her to apply for it and she got it. I thought, a bit unfair, that she got it because she was a female but since I came to the department I've realized that she's one of the best in her generation. But she had given me those signals that she was not going to continue, that she didn't want to and that she didn't have the drive. But she had that [[drive: my ref.]] I think she's one of the best in her age group. She was putting herself down, I've tried to tell her 'you gave me those signals that you weren't good enough, but you are, there is no question about it'".

The example should be studied in the light of the Swedish context which includes a recent initiative to raise the number of females at professor level as well as facilitating the transition from PhD exam to tenure (Bill 1994/

95: 164). This is to be done with the help of affirmative action measures and has led to a vivid debate about the competence of women being employed under these conditions. The fear of many is that women will be seen as less competent and as having been offered positions or scholarships only because they are women[10]. Such arguments rest on the notion of meritocracy and reveal that the dominant discourse of female researchers is that they are inferior researchers compared to their male counterparts. In other words, if meritocracy is the basis for advancement in the academic system then women should be able to make it on their own as well as men. If they do not make it on their own, it is because they are not good enough. The notion of meritocracy has been widely criticized during the last few decades and social scientific studies of science have highlighted the social dimensions in the reward and evaluation systems of science. Feminists have pointed at the impact of the "old boys network" for future career development and concepts such as "glass ceiling" or "subtle discrimination" are well established in the field of gender in higher education (Harding 1986, Caplan 1994, Long and Fox. 1995, Mackinnon 1997, Husu 2000).

In this quote Irene is very keen on stressing her position in relation to her colleague. It becomes obvious that she perceives herself as the older and more experienced researcher in relation to her colleague "[…] I've realized that she's one of the best in her generation." Or "[…] I think she's one of the best in her age group". At a first glance she appears to be very supportive of her colleague. "She was putting herself down, I've tried to tell her 'you gave me those signals that you weren't good enough, but you are, there is no question about it'. These lines also reveal that she constructs herself in the position as the wiser, more experienced researcher who encourages her younger colleague to pursue an academic career. It is tempting to stop the analysis here and conclude that she is supporting her colleague but at the same time constructing her as less competent and inferior to herself. That would be to ignore the issue of subject positions[11] and the complexities of it. If considering the lines again it becomes obvious that the tone is quite paternalistic, consequently the female researcher has taken the subject position of a (paternalistic) male researcher when explaining gender differences in scientific careers. She constructs herself as superior to her female colleague and constructs her colleague as feminine and inferior to her. This is not as contradictory as it sounds; it can be interpreted as one strategy for constructing herself more positively in a discourse where femininity is devalued. In addition it is important to remember that since academia is male-dominated, both historically and in its dominant discourses, there are no subject positions available to women academics unless they construct them themselves. This can be hard to accomplish without support.

In many areas the demands for equality between women and men in contemporary western societies have stimulated the processes of a reformulation of gender identities of both women and men. The interview excerpts above illustrate that gender differences in scientific careers are still explained in ways that reproduce gender hierarchy. Stanley from department B was asked the same question about gender differences in academic careers as Irene. Stanley has several children and his wife is also a researcher. He is ambivalent towards the effect of gender on scientific careers.

"Well, it's a world of old men, doing research, or at least has been. Women who continue as researchers, they have to show "fighting spirit", be really, [good: my ref.] they have to work even harder [than men: my ref.], it's sad but that's the way it is. I mean, it's not the way I want it to be. One can see how many PhDs there are as compared to doctoral students at the department. If considering sex distribution. It's probably fifty-fifty [[women and men: my ref.]] at doctoral student level but not at PhD level. But I believe we have a lot more female doctoral students compared to chemistry and organic chemistry, I'm not sure they have any females at all, well, maybe a few anyway. Why is it like that? It shouldn't be like that."

Stanley refers to the concept "a world of old men" in academia when explaining gender differences in scientific careers. The reasons for gender differences in scientific careers are thus deferred to processes within academia, which can be seen in light of the previous quotes. This is even more interesting when considering the researchers' family situation; researchers without children were more inclined to stress the importance of having children as an explanation than was the researcher who had children and who pointed at several different difficulties, the family situation being one of them. The quote also reveals that Stanley is part of the category that he refers to as oppressive, however, in a different age and power position. He is also keen to emphasize his dislike, which makes his argument a bit defensive: "it's sad but that's the way it is. I mean, it's not the way I want it to be". The first part of the sentence also reveals an element of acceptance: "it's sad but that's the way it is". The concept of "a world old men" appears several times when discussing reasons for gender differences in scientific careers. The following quote offers further insights into what is implied in this concept.

"It used to be easier for men to get tenure, that was what the study by Agnes Wold showed [...] I don't know whether it' stills true but that's what it showed. I don't know, but it seems as if women who want to have an academic career have to work so hard, on the other hand it should be like that for us too. One can hope that the problems are due to generational differences, but I'm afraid they're not. I fear that it's something you learn from older colleagues and you take after their values. You become like them even though you didn't think like that from the beginning[...]. It is a world of old men, they have all the high positions. From the beginning you're so self-centered and determined to do your own business but then you attend meetings, meet people and hear how they talk. Then you see how it is."

In this quote we can see that Stanley refers to a study, which states that nepotism, and sexism effects grant distribution in the life sciences. He expresses doubts about the relevance of the study "I don't know whether it' stills true but that's what it showed." A bit later in the quote he states: "[...] on the other hand it should be like that for us too". This implies that he is aware of the inequalities of the system, though he is ambivalent towards his position in it. He also refers to socialization processes and there is a bit of self-victimization in it implying that he himself is exposed to the patriarchal structures "You become like them even though you didn't think like that from the beginning[...] It is a world of old men, they have all the high positions". On the other hand we can see that he is in the process of internalizing their views: "You become like them even though you didn't think like that from the beginning". Stanley is ambivalent throughout the interview. He appears to be in a transitional period between, on the one hand keeping his distance to the system and being able to reflect critically over it On the other hand he is on his way to being socialized into the system, realizing that he is inferior to the privileged group. He also realizes that in order to belong to this group he has to pay the price, to "become like them". To "become like them" also appears to include a denial of gender inequality in academia, since it is highly unlikely that someone in the privileged group would openly declare that they had reached their position due to positive discriminating practices. His position, between criticizing and internalizing the dominant discourse of gender in academia, may be one explanation for his ambivalence towards the relevance of gender inequality in academia.

If we explore the concept of "old men" in the quote we can see that masculinities, seniority and academic position construct the group that holds the regime of truth of gender differences in academic careers in academia. This construction also implies that its binary opposition is different types of femininities. Thus, we can say that the groups of older men and younger men mutually reinforce each other since a major way of constructing masculinities is to compare with other forms of masculinities and to negate femininity (Collinson and Hearb 1994). For women to belong to this group they would have to change subject position; however, the price they would have to pay would most certainly be much higher since they would have to break considerably more normative rules as compared to men that enter this group.

Conclusions

As pointed out earlier it is highly unlikely that someone would openly declare women as less suited for pursuing an academic career. Still, gender differences in scientific careers based on gender inequality persist. In this article I have studied ways of reproducing gender inequality within the discourse of equality at two different Swedish university departments in the same area of biology. The results of the study indicate that the interviewed researchers at the departments are very keen to speak within the dominant discourse of gender equality operating on a general level of society. Yet, when making sense of gender differences in scientific careers, they tend to reproduce gender hierarchy, though in more subtle ways. One example is the exclusionary practices that seem to be at work. Women tend to be excluded, either by being constructed as problematic and lacking important qualities for succeeding in academia or by being constructed as different and sometimes overvalued as compared to men, however, both ways are exclusionary. There is also a tendency to individualize gender differences in scientific careers. Focus is often put on processes outside academia such as inequalities within families.

Another finding was that different forms of paternalism coexisted with the discourse of gender equality. By internalizing superiority as in the case of Irene in relation to her female colleague or by internalizing inferiority as in the case of Stanley in relation to the "world of old men" the gender order was reproduced when making sense of gender differences in academic careers. Thus, it appears to be more rewarding for researchers (male and female) to internalize the dominant views of gender rather than contest them and this seems to reinforce the "self-reproductive" tendencies in the academic system. By internalizing the regime of truth of femininity and masculinity the researchers can reproduce the symbolic order of gender in academia and still speak within the dominant discourse of gender equality. Thus, they construct themselves as "gender neutral", "good" researchers. Gender differences based on gender inequality in scientific careers becomes something that is outside the norm of gender equality in the Swedish university system[12]. Gender inequality is then constructed as something "abnormal" or at least something that happens at other departments or universities.

The lack of available subject positions for women academics, and the hard work of constructing such alternative positions, is an obstacle for women academics to support each other. The absence of subject positions for women, combined with the often unreasonably high expectations on women to support other women, are factors that further complicate how women researchers perceive other women researchers. As pointed out earlier, it is very hard to avoid making gender since it is a major way of categorize and making sense of our daily lives. In order to stop producing and reproducing hierarchical relations between femininities and masculinities we need to further examine how we create and maintain the symbolic order of gender when making sense of different situations and relations related to everyday academic working life.

Notes

1. Acknowledgments: I thank Nora Räthzel and Elin Kvist (Department of Sociology) and Maria Carbin (Department of Political Science, Umeå University, Sweden) for valuable comments during the process of writing this work.
2. In this article "scientific", "academic" and "research" career are used synonymously. They imply that the researcher has completed his/her PhD and continued to work with research or research related work within academia, or found research related work outside academia.
3. In this article "gender order" implies an asymmetrical relation between femininity and masculinity where the feminine is devalued in relation to the masculine.
4. There is an ongoing debate about the usefulness and implications of the distinction between (social) gender and (biological) sex. This will not be further elaborated in this article, however, for an introduction to the debate, please consider *Gender Trouble*, Judith Butler 1992: 3–44.
5. For an overview please, see *Representations and signifying practices*, S. Hall 1997:15–74.
6. When a number of discursive events, texts or practices, share the same style or refer to the same strategy they are said by Foucault to belong to the same *discursive formation* (Foucault in Hall 1997:44).
7. For a further elaboration of such approaches

please consider "Talking about Careers and Gender identities: A Discourse Analysis Perspective", Harriet Marshall and Margret Wetherell in *The Social Identity of Women* (eds.) S. Skevington and D. Baker 1989.
8. Here I am influenced by Donna Haraways concept *Situated Knowledge's* (1996).
9. The departments have previously been described and analyzed by sociological and bibliometric means in "Mapping gender differences in scientific careers in social and bibliometric space" *Science technology and human values.* Vol. 26. No. 2 Spring 2002:167–190.
10. An analysis of the media discourse that followed after the bill was passed revealed that these types of arguments were very common and that male academics, with one exception, represented those who were negative to the bill. On the positive side were women and men as well as academics and non-academics (Bondestam 1999).
11. Discourses produce subjects (for example the madman or the criminal), however they also produce places for the subject where the discourse makes most sense. In other words discourses produce different subject positions through which the subject can make meaning (Hall 1997: 56).
12. Gender inequality as a contradiction to the Swedish "norm of equality" has previously been elaborated by Rönnblom et al. in *Jämställdhet, retorik som Praktik?* (1999).

References

Acker, J. 1992: *Gendering Organizational Theory. Gendering Organizational Analysis*. Mills, A.J. and Tancred, P. (eds.). London: Sage. 248–261.
de Beauvoir, S. 1949: *Le deuxième sexe*. Paris: Les Editions des Minuit.
Bondestam, F. 1999: Positiv Särbehandling i Akademin – tjugofem år av ideologi, retorik och praktik. Unpublished Essay. Department of Sociology. Uppsala University, Sweden.
Butler, J. 1992: *Gender trouble: feminism and the subversion of identity*. New York: Routledge.
Caplan, P. 1994: *Lifting a Ton of Feathers: A Woman's Guide for Surviving in the Academic World*. Canada. University of Toronto Press.
Cockburn, C. 1991: *In the Way of Women*. London: Macmillan.
Collinson, D. and Hearb, J. 1994: Naming Men as Men; Implications for Work, Organization and Management. *Gender Work & Organization* (1).
Cole, J. and Zuckerman, H. 1991: Marriage, Motherhood, and Research Performance within The Outer Circle. In: *Women in the Scientific Community*. Cole, J. Zuckerman, H. and J. Bruer, (eds.). New York: Norton. 159–169.
Davies, C. 1996: The Sociology of Professions and the Profession of Gender. *Journal of British Sociological Association* 30(4): 661–678.
Davis, D.E. and Astin, H.S. 1990: Life Cycle, Career Patterns and Gender Stratification in Academe. In: *Breaking Myths and Exposing Truths. Storming the Tower. Women in the academic world*. Stiver Lie, S. and O'Leary, V. (eds.). London: Kogan Page. 89–107.
Elgquist-Saltzman, I. 1994: Straight roads and winding tracks. In: *Gender and Education in a Life Perspective, Lessons from Scandinavia*, Bjeren, G. and Elgquist-Saltzman I. (eds.). England: Avebury. 7–17.
Foucault, M. 1980: *Power/Knowledge*. Brighton: Harvester.
Fox, M.F. and Faver, C.A. 1985: Men, Women and Publication Productivity: Patterns among Social Work, Academics. *The Sociological Quarterly*. 26(4)537–549.
Gherardi, S. 1994: The Gender We Think, The Gender We Do in Our Everyday Organizational Lives. *Human Relations* 47(6), 591–609.
Gherardi, S. 1995: *Gender, Symbolism and Organizational Cultures*. London: Sage.
Government Bill (1994/95): 164.
Hall, S. 1997: *Representation, Cultural Representations and Signifying Practices*. London: Sage. 13–74.
Haraway, D. 1996: Situated knowledges; The Science Question in Feminism and the privilege of the partial perspective. In: *Feminism and Science*. Keller, E.F. and Longino H.E. (eds.). Oxford: Oxford University Press. 249–263.
Harding, S. 1986: *The Science Question in Feminism*. Milton Keynes: Open University Press.
Hirdman, Y. 1988: Genussystemet. Reflektioner kring kvinnors social underordning. *Kvinnovetenskaplig tidskrift* 1988/3.
Human and Development Report. Gender and Human development, UNDP, Oxford University Press (1995).
Husu, L. 2000: Gender Equality in Finnish academia: contradictions and Interventions. In: *Hard Work in the Academy*. Fogelberg, P., Hearn, J., Husu, L. and Mankkinen, T. (eds.). Helsinki: Helsinki University Press.
Kanter, R. M. 1977: *Men and Women of the Corporation*. New York: Basic Books.
Katila, S. and Meriläinen, S. 1999: A Serious Researcher of Just Another Nice Girl? Doing Gender in a maledominated scientific community. *Gender, Work and Organization*. 6(3). July.
Keller, E.F. 1985: *Reflections on Gender and Science*. New Haven: Yale University Press.
Kyvik, S. 1991: *Productivity in Academia: Scientific Publishing at Norwegian Universities*. Rådet for samfunnsvitenskapelig forsking NAVF: Universitetsforlag. 186–224.
Long J.S. 1993: *Women in Science*. Part 2. The Impact Enigma – Why Women Biochemists' papers are more cited than men's. Current Comments. Institute for Scientific Information. 11. Mars 15. 259–269.
Long, J.S. and Fox, M.F. 1995: Scientific Careers: Universalism and Particularism. *Annu. Rev. Sociol*. 21:45–71.

Luukonen-Gronow, T. 1987: University Career Opportunities for Women in Finland in the 1980s, *Acta Sociologica* 1987(30), 2:193–206.

Mackinnon, A. 1997: *Love and freedom; The Professional Women and the Reshaping of Personal Life*. Cambridge: Cambridge University Press.

Marshall, H. and Wetherell, M. 1989: Talking about career and gender Identities: A discourse analysis perspective. In: *The Social Identity of Women*. Skevington, S. and Baker, D. (eds.). London: Sage. 106–129.

National Agency for Higher Education. 2001. Yearbook.

Sonnert, G. and Holton, G, 1995: *Gender Differences in Scientific Careers*. New Jersey: Rutgers University Press.

Stolte-Heiskanen, V. 1991: Handmaidens of the 'knowledge class': women in science in Finland. In: *Women in Science: Token Women or Gender Equality?* Stolte-Heiskanen, V. and Furst-Dolic (eds.). Oxford: Berg.

Tollin, K. 1998: Kommunalråds och Kommunchefers syn på jämställdhet. Jämställdhet – Retorik som Praktik? *Länsstyrelsen Västerbottenslän*. 26–39.

Peters, H.P.F. and Vanraan, A.F.J. 1991: Structuring scientific activity by co-author analysis – an exercise on a university faculty level. *Scientometrics* 20: 235–255.

Rönnblom, M. *et al.* 1999: Jämställdhet – Retorik som Praktik? *Länsstyrelsen Västerbottenslän*.

Wager, M. 1994: *Construction of femininity of academic women; Continuity between Private and Professional Identity*. Diss. Helsinki.

Wahl, A., Holgersson, C. and Höök, P. 1998: *Ironi & Sexualitet om ledarskap och kön*. Stockholm: Carlssons Bokförlag.

Winnifred, T. and Hamilton, G. 1988: *Gender Bias in Scholarship: The Pervasive Prejudice*. Waterloo, Canada: Wilfrid Laurier University Press.

Wold, A. and Wennerås, C. 1997: Nepotism and sexism in peer-review. *Nature*. 387: (6631) May 22. 341–343.